10638162

Save Your
Marriage
in Five
Minutes a Day

PART 1

Five-Minute Strategies to Keep the Spark Alive

Chapter 1

Let's Get Physical

Strolling through your neighborhood, have you ever smiled to see an elderly couple holding hands? Perhaps you sighed and said to yourself, "Still in love after all these years." That couple's longevity is no accident. They demonstrate a key element to making a marriage last: uncomplicated, everyday affection. Daily touching between you and your partner doesn't necessarily have to be sexual. A pat on the hand during a talk can signify understanding; a cuddle on the couch can bring a feeling of togetherness. In just five minutes—or even less!—a small physical gesture can remind your spouse that he is valued, or that she is not alone.

When Affection Fades

Why do we need to be reminded of so seemingly simple an act? Unfortunately, as our marriages mature and life becomes complicated by careers and children, successes and defeats, daily warmth is often eclipsed by chronic or intermittent stress and distractions. The "Honey, I'm home!" scenario of the wife happily kissing her man in the foyer is now usurped by a yell from the kitchen: "Honey, can you take the dog out while I finish dinner?" In our society, we all seem to be high functioning; we do it all and try to never forget to kiss our kids' boo boos and hug them daily. Even so, affection for our spouses too often falls by the wayside. In an unintentional evolution, the young couple that couldn't keep their hands off one another becomes ships passing—and passing out—in the night.

A marriage lacking in daily love can feel like a well-oiled machine that merely gets the job done. Where's the joy in that? What's more, as life's inevitable difficulties arise, spouses who are unused to being mutually affectionate may miss out on a sustaining source of comfort. You need continuity of affection to keep you and your spouse bonded; without it, you risk being together, but feeling alone.

Infuse Your Marriage with Affection

Offering your spouse a daily kiss, hug, or backrub reminds her of your devotion, and reinstates your sense of being "in this together." The good news? Five minutes a day is all you need to restore friendly affection to your marriage, a small effort that leads to a huge emotional payoff. Most of us would *like* to be more affectionate. The key is having the discipline to *take the time* to reach out for our partners as we rush through our busy days.

Below are some hypothetical affection forks in the road. Put yourself in these shoes. Which choice would you likely make?

Ignoring Affection Opportunity	Embracing Affection Opportunity
It's late, and your wife is putting away the leftovers from dinner. You say goodnight from the hall and go into the den, where you promptly fall asleep in front of the TV.	It's late, and your wife is putting away the leftovers from dinner. As she puts the plastic wrap in the drawer, you come up from behind and wrap your arms around her. You could say how much you appreciated dinner, but perhaps your gesture says it all.
Your husband is in his office having a heated phone call with his mother. You stand just out of sight in order to overhear what they are fighting about.	Your husband is in his office having a heated phone call with his mother. Not wanting to intrude, but still show support, you walk behind him and give him a brief shoulder rub before leaving the vicinity.
Your husband is a grumpy shopper who needs new pants desperately. As you quickly walk through the mall, he lags behind like a reluctant teen. You fume.	Your husband is a grumpy shopper who needs new pants desperately. You match his reluctant stride and put your arm around his waist, your hand in his back pocket, like a teen. You both crack up.
It's 7 A.M. and you and your wife are scrambling to get everyone out the door. You give her a quick kiss on the cheek—your customary move—and you're out the door.	It's 7 A.M. and you and your wife are scrambling to get everyone out the door. In front of the kids, you scoop her up into your arms and twirl her around. Everyone begins the day laughing.

Given the fact that one in three couples believe their marriage is at risk of "going stale," choosing to engage in simple, quick acts of love is a smart and easy way to stay connected, to fan the flame. Interestingly, physical affection is habitual and reciprocal: The more you touch your spouse, the more she will be reminded and encouraged to do the same.

Affection During Conflict

Physical affection can also be a powerful way to smooth over the inevitable rough spots every marriage encounters.

When we argue, expressing our feelings and viewpoints through words can be limiting. We hear what we want to hear, we don't listen at all, or we tune out something said in a berating tone. But who would argue with a hug? A hug or a hand reached out as a peace offering is straightforward and irrefutable. Interestingly, in a 2004 study of forty-nine newlywed couples, John Gottman and Janice Driver discovered that daily positive interactions contribute to a couple's ability to use affection and humor during an argument. In the study, the female participants were more affectionate when the men acted playfully throughout the day.

SAY THIS

"We may not see eye to eye on this issue, but I still love you. Let's cuddle for a few minutes on the couch and then reapproach this tomorrow."

I advise the couples that I counsel to ignore grandma's advice to never go to bed angry. Often, it is wiser to take a break to regroup—and to let those high emotions simmer down. (Not to mention the fact that you need to get sufficient sleep.) Instead of fighting all night, agree to go to bed without resolution, but then soften those remaining harsh feelings by engaging in your affectionate nightly routine. Kiss each other before you fall asleep; tell your spouse you love him; spoon each other for a few moments. If you aren't normally affectionate at bedtime, make an extra effort to reach out to your partner despite any hurt feelings. This brief physical contact will increase the likelihood of a resolution come morning.

An Affection Mismatch

Despite the fact that most couples find themselves aligned in many ways—they share the same value system, have similar views on money, both love old Westerns—when it comes to daily affection, there is sometimes a mismatch. Some people are simply less physically inclined than others. Perhaps you grew up in a family that didn't show their love through physical contact? Maybe a boundary was crossed long ago and that abuse still resonates when love is offered? Whatever the reason for you or your partner's discomfort with overt displays, a happy marriage depends on finding a space that satisfies both people.

> ### *Extra Credit*
> The next Saturday morning when you can sleep in, curl up against your spouse for a few moments and see if it leads to a good cuddle or—even better—satisfying sex.

The more affection-inclined of the two of you may feel neglected if hugs and kisses are few and far between. At the same time, if your reticent spouse feels crowded by sitting on his lap uninvited or wanting to kiss when she's not in the mood, unintentional smothering may result. Five minutes of daily warmth can still work for such a couple—but the timing and approach are crucial. If you crave affection and feel it's missing, don't wait for your spouse to offer it. Reach out in moments that are relaxed. Without calling attention to it ("See, this isn't so bad!"), or implying guilt ("Why don't we hold hands at the movies *for once?*"), lightly take your partner's hand for a few minutes, and then let it go. The key is no pressure, no guilt. Tread lightly.

SUSAN & ANDREW'S STORY

Susan came from an Italian home that prized self-expression. Her mother insisted on making Sunday dinners and all hell broke loose if all five children did not show up and eat until they burst. After dinner, Susan's dad would put on the opera records and the entire family would sing. After much eating, kissing, and hugging, everyone went home.

Susan married Andrew, a boy from a Connecticut family of conservative New England stock. Andrew's family demonstrated affection by showing up, not showing off. There were no public displays, no excessive crying, cursing, hitting, or kissing. At first Andrew felt relieved to be in Susan's world, but it eventually became at bit much—too demanding, too out of control.

After some time, when Susan asked for a kiss, or took Andrew's hand he said, "Stop being a baby. We are adults with children of our own. Grow up."

Susan decided to help her marriage toward the physicality she craved. Sitting together over coffee, she began: "Andrew, what do you mean when you tell me to stop being a baby?"

"You know what I mean; don't play dumb."

"I don't understand. What is the connection between asking for a kiss and being a baby?"

"Kissing is for kids or to get laid. Your family is over the top when it comes to this stuff."

"What are your thoughts on kissing? Why do you think it's just for kids?"

"Well, when I was a kid, my Aunt Beatrice would run into my house yelling at the top of her lungs, 'Gimme a kiss, gimme a kiss!' I felt trapped, humiliated, and disgusted. No one else ever behaved that way in my childhood."

"Andrew. I don't want to trap you or embarrass you when I ask for a kiss. Do you believe me?"

"Yes."

"Good because when I ask for a kiss it is strictly to feel the warmth of your body and the comfort of your arms. I love you so much."

"Me too."

By exploring the root of Andrew's discomfort, and by allowing one another to voice their motivating influences, Susan and Andrew moved closer to a space where they both felt comfortable. If you and your spouse differ on how frequently to offer hugs and kisses, answers may lie in an exploration of the past. When you discover the personal meaning behind your spouse's intolerance for closeness, you can then build a bridge from your point of view to his.

SAY THIS

"When you were growing up, did you ever see your parents embrace? Did their affection (or lack thereof) carry over to how they treated you?"

Remember: The more you offer, the more affection you'll eventually receive. Touch is a basic need. The urge is there, just waiting to be tapped into. From birth, touch, along with sleep and nourishment, allow us to thrive as infants, and that same tactile need is present throughout our lives. We are meant to stroke and be stroked. And, for five minutes a day, this is such a simple way to fulfill that urge and remind yourself that you and your partner belong together.

Offering your spouse affection through touch is a simple— and quick—way to cement your love on a daily basis. A tender gesture only takes a few minutes, but like a stone thrown into a pond, it will reverberate throughout your day. And, in your darker moments, taking five minutes to physically shore up your marriage will let the light back in.

- Hugging is a universal source of comfort. It conveys reassurance, togetherness, and confirms the fact that the two of you will stand strong no matter what storms may rage. Notice when your partner seems down or pensive and offer a calming embrace.
- Embracing your partner from behind is a nondemanding gesture that is a token of your warmth. More casual than a hug, this is a reminder that says, "Although we race through our separate days, you are the one I will always come back to." Surprise your spouse (but be careful not to startle!) with a cuddle from behind while she is engaged in some mundane task, like dishes or sorting the mail.
- Whether it's a quick peck, or a long and sultry make-out session, kissing gets your blood racing. Nothing is more intimate—not even sex. Over time, it's easy to forget its power as we race out the door or fall gratefully into our beds. Remind yourself to kiss your partner goodbye and hello and anytime you think of it in between. In a more intimate setting, slow things down to a pleasurable simmer by just kissing for five minutes.

- Holding hands is an uncomplicated sign of your togetherness. Suitable for both private and public settings, holding hands is an announcement to the world that you belong together. Reaching for your spouse's hand may also take you back to those first few dates where his touch sent sparks flying. Holding hands can also be used as a private language—a silent gesture of support when you know your spouse is nervous in front of his boss, or when her mother says something critical.
- Linking arms is charmingly old-fashioned and shows that you lean on each other. While walking together, take his arm or offer her your arm and notice an instant feeling of togetherness. If you and your partner don't enjoy holding hands, this gesture is a great alternative.
- Turn your usual TV time into a physical encounter by cuddling on the couch. Rather than sitting in separate seats, or putting the bowl of popcorn between you, just plop down and snuggle up. This turns what could have been an average evening into a warm shared experience.
- Before you sleep or when you wake, spoon your partner. You will drift off to sleep sharing the warmth of each other's bodies. Spooning can often lead to sex; the feeling of the full length of your spouse's body pressed up against yours can be hard to resist.
- Offering your loved one a back or shoulder rub—one that's not too hard and not too soft—can ease her tension. This is an unselfish act that is usually appreciated beyond measure, especially if it's unsolicited. And don't forget foot massages, which can be surprisingly sensual.

Chapter 2

Tokens of Affection

A recent study of 121 couples ranging in age from eighteen to fifty-nine years revealed that the more committed the couple was, the more often they made use of certain behaviors to show their dedication. It was found that one of these behaviors is "Offering Tangible Reminders," such as giving gifts and notes. Flowers or a card for no reason are two examples of the unlimited ways you can remind your lover that he is cherished. And gestures don't have to cost money or smack of romance to elicit a smile. If you know your wife hates to miss *Mad Men*, DVR-ing the show when she works late is proof that you are thinking of her. Or if your husband loves *The Economist* magazine, for example, ask him to let you know when an article really speaks to him. You would love to read it also.

These actions often take less than five minutes and benefit your marriage not only because they make your partner happy, but because they are self-empowering. Generosity is a gift to the giver as well as the recipient. The anticipation of presenting your partner with coveted concert tickets can provide hours of pleasure gleaned from just five minutes spent on Ticketmaster.com! Thoughtful gestures sow fertile ground for a happy union and, if such offerings become part of your marriage, the give-and-take will keep your love in a steady state of creativity.

Complexities of Giving

A simple idea can become surprisingly complex when you consider: 1) knowing what it is that will bring your spouse pleasure, and 2) refraining from proffering something you desire which may or may not be your partner's cup of tea. If you are attracted to someone whose interests vary greatly from your own, gift giving can be challenging, but those differences can keep you mutually intrigued and surprised by each other's individuality. As the years unfold, layers peel away revealing progressively more and more about the person with whom you share your life. So, if your man is a tech geek and you prefer letters to e-mails, can you remain sensitive to this polarity? What he considers meaningful may be foreign to you. (An iPhone upgrade seems so unromantic!) Likewise, he may never imagine that what you desire is an unplugged evening together.

> ### *Extra Credit*
> Pay attention: What makes him happy? What past gestures have meant the most to her? Be mindful of each other and the small acts that count will easily come to mind.

Adding to the challenge of finding the needle-in-the-haystack gift is that many people give what they themselves would want. We all need refreshing changes, to step out of the routine of everyday life. An elegant evening of champagne and flowers in a downtown hotel may be your dream date. So, you arrange just such an experience and he responds with, "Why'd you go and waste all this money?" Your spirits deflate. But think about it: Who was the surprise really for? Your thrifty, alcohol-adverse man? A closer look points the finger at the true target recipient: you. No wonder he wasn't moved. This phenomenon often happens when one partner is trying to watch his weight and the other unthinkingly shows up with a "surprise" favorite meal or dessert. The Ben and Jerry's you devoured when you were eight months pregnant is no longer a thoughtful nod—it's diet sabotage. Below are some strategies for thoughtful gift-giving

- **Listening:** Keep an ear to the ground for clues as to what your partner desires. His admiration of a song on the radio could be the motivation that sends you straight to Amazon.com for the artist's CD.
- **Avoid Assumptions:** Just because she's a woman doesn't mean she loves perfume and not all men like televisions (although many do). Look deeper into personal gift giving.
- **Creativity Counts:** Thoughtfulness and imagination signify more than money spent. Anyone (with means) can buy a bracelet at the local department store. Resetting her grandmother's diamond in a custom-designed setting is priceless.

Beyond the Material

Often the gifts we crave do not come ensconced in wrapping paper. Ask any busy mother of young children what she desires and it's probably an hour devoted to her own needs. Or, consider your partner's mood the first five minutes after he arrives home from work. You may be eager to regale him with details of the rude plumber, the unexpected tax bill, or other daily inconveniences, but by choosing instead to offer him five minutes of quiet or a funny story, you are giving him a thoughtful gift. These acts of generosity take little time and cost nothing, yet they imbue your marriage with a feeling of teamwork.

SAY THIS

"I have enjoyed every gift you have ever given me. But, now that we are so busy with work and family, all I really want is you. When can we set aside a time to be alone together?"

LARRY & MARIA'S STORY

Larry and Maria were married for two years and she frequently bought him little gifts. He believed they were an expression of her fear; that Maria thought if she stopped showering him with affection, he would leave her. For Maria, the gifts were actually her way of showing Larry that she was thinking of him when they were apart.

Larry decided to give Maria feedback on this problem without hurting her feelings or shaming her. So he planned to speak to her about it after a day of hiking in the Adirondack Mountains. They were staying at a bed and breakfast, and after a gracious meal, Larry asked Maria to take a walk in the night air. Nervous, but determined, he began, "Maria, I want to speak to you about something that is bothering me. Are you up to hearing about it?"

"Sure, go ahead."

"Well, I know how much you love buying me gifts, and I understand that you are showing me how much you love me. But for me they are becoming clutter. I would appreciate another kind of token of love."

"I'm a little hurt, but this is obviously important to you. Keep going."

"I don't want to hurt you, but I do want to give you feedback that can strengthen our love. For me, a way to show you care would be to allow me to watch the football games for the entire season without getting upset. I ask for time with no guilt to watch the games on Sundays, some Saturday evenings, and some Monday evenings. Of course if something else comes up during a scheduled game, I promise to be a good sport and complain as little as possible."

"This is a big request, Larry. Give me some time to think about it."

Larry's calm explanation of his feelings eventually convinced Maria that her well-intentioned gift giving was missing the mark. This new way of thinking let her show Larry how much she loved him without spending money or giving him items that complicated his life. Instead of brooding while Larry watches his games, she now gives him the five-minute gift of sitting down with him, hearing the latest exciting play, and then leaving him to pursue her own interests.

It can be difficult to express what you want from your partner (especially if she continually misses the mark) without feeling needy, ungrateful, or selfish.

But though you may wish she could read your mind, a better bet is to be tactful, yet direct. A quick dialogue about what you really desire can promote greater understanding between you and your spouse.

Use Your Senses

How are we capable of perceiving our own experiences of happiness as well as our partner's? An imaginative approach to thinking about all that you can offer your partner is to use your five senses. Neurologist Antonio Damasio suggests the image of an ongoing "movie in the brain" that constitutes consciousness: an illustration which demonstrates a realization "that the movie has as many sensory tracks as our nervous system has sensory portals—sight, sound, taste, and olfaction, touch, inner senses, and so on." Happiness can be experienced from just one or two of these sensory portals or from most of them.

Consider devoting each day of the week to either sight, hearing, smell, taste, or touch. This offers a framework for giving and inspires creativity!

Sight

Use your sense of sight to study what gestures elicit happiness in your partner. Does he light up when you give him tickets to your local baseball team's opening night? Does he beam at the idea of an intimate kid-free evening together? Watch, too, to see what doesn't inspire a smile. (How about that necktie you gave him as an anniversary gift last year?) Then, consider what visual treats he enjoys. Does he take pleasure in the sunset? Perhaps drive one evening to an overlook? Or, is it *you* he wants to see in his button-down shirt with nothing on underneath?

Hearing

Listening is a most important gift. Tuning in—with no expectations, interruptions, or judgment—is crucial for long-term contentment. Listen for signals as to what would bring your partner even more delight. What does she exclaim over when talking to others: a friend's silver earrings or the time you brought home a bunch of wildflowers? Also, think about gifts devoted to the ear. Are tickets to the symphony or a 1970s rock band something she would enjoy, or alternatively a quiet evening away from the usual cacophony of your life?

Smell

Of all the senses, smell is the most intimately connected to emotions. Just a passing whiff of a long-ago lover's scent can rocket you back in time. Pheromones, those under-the-radar chemicals that the nose detects, play a key role in choosing a mate. Use this sense to create new memories by giving the heady gift of flowers or perfume. Another alluring nod to olfactory stimulation is baking bread or a pie (or a curry or marinara) that you know elicits childhood memories. This shows your partner that you care about him, remember his stories, and that your present life is as comforting as the best parts of his childhood. As your home fills with aromas, so does appreciation from your mate.

Taste

Similarly, taste provides opportunity for caring gestures. Five-minute offerings are no further than your local deli or coffee shop. Show up with your wife's favorite scone or a yummy coffee drink. Breakfast in bed is a soothing way to start the day—and it only takes five minutes to make eggs and toast. Taste can play an intriguing role in the bedroom as well. Some people are excited by the salty taste of a lover's skin on a hot day. Others enjoy a more creative approach of flavored oils or lubricants.

Touch

Being affectionate is crucial. Touch is such a basic and effective way to show love and attraction. Offer backrubs and hugs throughout the day. A momentary handhold on a walk is a friendly reminder of your togetherness. Pay attention, though. There will be times when your partner may not want to be touched. Stressed out after a frustrating conference call, he may need to just be alone or go for a stress-relieving jog. In such a case, your gift to him is the gift of space.

Five-Minute Strategies

Five minutes a day is nothing. You likely take that much time to look for your keys or shave. What could be more important than devoting the same amount of time to offering your spouse a daily affirmation? Through these gestures, much comfort and pleasure can be found. Challenge your ingenuity by devising personal ways to make your partner smile. The possibilities are endless!

- Talk about the gifts that each of you enjoy. Take five minutes to be open with each other and admit that all you really want is an evening alone with him or that this year for your birthday, you're hoping for an iPad rather than jewelry. Honest communication lays the groundwork for successful gift giving.
- Arrive home on a random day with an offering you know will be appreciated. Does she love flowers? Does he collect paperweights? Giving a present that proves you know your partner well increases intimacy. And, a surprise present—even if it's modest—only serves to heighten the pleasure.
- Capitalize on your lover's fondness of food/drink. Is he watching his weight? A low-fat coffee drink may be appreciated. Is she homesick? Buy or make enchiladas that remind her of home.
- Complete a dreaded chore. Taking the recycling out to the street or scrubbing that grease-encrusted pan may not seem romantic, but you are actually giving your spouse the gift of time to pursue more pleasurable activities.
- To charm him out of a bad mood give him the gift of your smile and warmth. If you notice he's having a

tough day, take a few minutes to relay an amusing story you know he'll appreciate. Or, give him an unsolicited backrub so sensual he forgets his troubles altogether.

- Give thoughtful compliments. In less than a minute, you have the power to turn your spouse's gray Monday into a great start to the week. Notice something admirable about her and let her know—does she look pretty in that color? Does she cook the best eggs you've ever had? A well-placed compliment is something she will replay in her mind again and again with delight.

- Appreciate your partner's differences. Challenge yourself to give a reward that you yourself would not want and, frankly, do not understand. If you hate single malt scotch, but know your husband savors a glass on a winter evening, head to the liquor store. If you know your wife has always wanted a couples' massage, but the thought makes your eyes roll, make the appointment anyway. These gestures are gift-giving double-whammys that show you are willing to put your own opinions aside for your spouse's pleasure.

- Take the kids out of the house. Go out to the yard to throw the ball for a few minutes and let your spouse enjoy much-deserved quiet time. Especially if you have young children, a few minutes where there is no one underfoot is a precious gift.

- Be generous in bed. Put your partner's pleasure before your own; this gift will keep her smiling long after you're dressed. Sexual generosity fosters an atmosphere of goodwill in and out of the bedroom. Plus, generosity in bed may inspire your partner to return the favor next time.

Chapter 3

Creative Foreplay

Remember those first encounters when just the touch of your spouse's hand electrified your entire body? When a kiss could be felt in your toes? As time goes by, the heady spark of lustful sexual attraction fades from fireworks to a pleasant glow (or, in some cases, is extinguished entirely). What if I told you that in only five minutes a day you could recapture that initial excitement in a new form?

Imaginative foreplay goes beyond the bedroom—and it's something that everyone wants more of. In fact, a recent study of 152 couples in the *Journal of Sex Research* proves the importance of bringing more foreplay into your everyday life. It reported that survey takers' ideal desired extent of foreplay is "significantly longer than the actual duration for both genders." So take opportunities in your everyday life to imbue your relationship with a sexy vibe. It can vary from a stolen kiss to a meaningful glance across the dinner table.

Foreplay vs. Sex

Remember that scene in *Pretty Woman* where heart-of-gold hooker Julia Roberts refuses to kiss her handsome client? There's a reason for that. Kissing is more intimate than intercourse. Anyone can have sex, but foreplay is where we are vulnerable and shy—and also at our best. Foreplay is delicate; testing the waters to see what your lover responds to takes experimentation. When it works, it demonstrates that you and your partner know each other. Try titillating play for five minutes each day, and continue discovering more about the person you chose. It's an adventure that will pay off.

Engaging in inspired sensual banter can, in time, progress to a happy physical encounter. If you look to ancient Eastern philosophies, you'll discover the idea of prolonging orgasm for as long as possible, as ejaculation signifies the expenditure of a life force. This delay of ultimate gratification can be found in Chinese lore, Taoism, and Indian philosophy—as seen in the *Kama Sutra*. If you devote five minutes in the morning to foreplay, you'll carry that warm glow with you throughout the day, even as you carpool the kids, do the dishes, and pay the bills.

Vision and Intimacy

There are as many sex acts as there are grains of sand and we are all aroused differently. Innovative sexuality means being tuned into your partner's preferences. If you know that a bold make-out session up against a wall would excite him, pull him into an unused room during a party and surprise him. Or, maybe your partner is turned on by a more subtle approach. Perhaps a soft brush against her thigh as you reach across her lap can send a shiver down her spine. If you're not sure how to proceed, try one of the following ideas:

Bold	Subtle
Take his hand while watching TV and place it on your breast or upper thigh.	Hug him for longer than usual when you part. He'll remember the feeling of your body throughout the day.
When the kids leave the room for a minute, softly and deeply kiss her mouth.	Give her a heart-felt massage.
Send him an unexpected suggestive e-mail describing what you wish you were doing with/to him.	Instead of going into the bathroom to change, slowly dress or undress in front of him.
Take a blanket to a park and enjoy the envious looks as you kiss and cuddle.	Cook a seductive meal and then feed each other with your hands.

Remember: Getting an accurate read on your partner's mood can be just as important as the act itself. Even the boldest among us may not appreciate a surprise lap dance when we've just received the tax bill. That said, sometimes offering a spark of sensuality can shake a partner out of a glum state of mind, especially if humor is involved. Look before you leap. However, if your spouse says he's not in the right frame of mind use the rejection as an opportunity to strengthen your own boundaries so you are able to receive "no" without personalizing it. You have a lifetime of opportunities to keep the spark alive.

What If I'm Too Self-Conscious?

These suggestions may all sound well and good, but if your marriage has been rather chilly of late, everyday seductiveness may seem like too big a leap. You may feel self-conscious, overly dramatic, needy, or just plain childish to treat your ongoing relationship the way you would a first date or the beginning of a liaison where the chemistry is electric. You may be thinking: *What if he laughs at me?* Or, *What if she rejects my advances and I feel even more alone?* Start slowly and be honest. You may want to display this book and explain how committed you are to upgrading your marriage. Ask your spouse to be a good sport and join the adventure. Then, nuzzle his neck one morning over coffee (or use a similar subtle approach) and see what happens. If he resists or seems surprised, tease him into playing along. Over time, your advances may become welcome and reciprocated.

If there is anger or tension in the air, sparking some sexy heat can help to dissipate that negativity. Use creative fore-play to demonstrate that you are still attracted to your mate despite your differences. Every marriage experiences rough patches, but smoothing out a raw atmosphere with kisses and caresses can shore up a rocky phase.

Extra Credit

Great make-up foreplay can be as satisfying as make-up sex. End a fight with a passionate kiss or sensual backrub and watch negative feelings fade.

TOM & DAISY'S STORY

After a tense day as a securities trader, Tom arrived home exhausted. As soon as he walked in the door, his wife, Daisy, asked him to unplug the stuffed-up toilet. As he bent to his task, she became impassioned over the water spilling all over the bathroom floor. He erupted in fury and started to yell at her. He was upset that she couldn't show enthusiasm for all of the important things in life and yet was alive and awake over the water on the bathroom floor.

Tom's ardent wish for himself and Daisy (and his most preferred form of creative foreplay) is hysterical laughing over everyday absurdities. Initially, Daisy was his best audience, and their laughter inevitably led to the bedroom. But over time, Tom started to put Daisy's actions under a microscope, gauging just how inactive she was from moment to moment. Tom felt extremely unappreciated in his first family and unintentionally re-enacted the original drama with Daisy, thus getting the same outcome. In his eyes he was again faced with a disinterested loved one.

Tom believed that he was justifiably frustrated over his loss of a giggling, appreciative spectator, and that this caused foreplay in their marriage to become virtually nonexistent. From Daisy's viewpoint, she felt judged on a moment-by-moment basis. Tom's frustration only increased her self-consciousness.

The following day, Tom approached Daisy as she was getting dressed: "I am sorry that I got so angry last night."

"I am sorry that I got so uptight over the water on the floor."

"What were you so concerned about? It was actually a funny moment."

"Well, the baby took two hours to go to sleep. And just as she drifted off you came home and the water went splashing everywhere. I knew I was only going to sleep a few hours before she was up again, and I'm just exhausted. I know how irritable I become when I am sleep deprived. Do you understand?"

"Yes, but, from my point of view I also came home stressed and was looking to get cozy with you and the baby where I would have no one yelling at me. I wanted a few jokes, some light-hearted fun. Instead, with all the yelling, cursing, and demanding, it almost felt like I was back on the trading room floor."

"I'm so sorry, Tom."

Tom and Daisy's resolution is a stepping-stone back to the sexy, laughter-filled early days of their marriage. It is a matter of mutual understanding while both are trying to keep their heads above water. If you and your spouse are finding it difficult to create everyday passion due to stress and arguments, start the conversation by saying something like, "I know things have been difficult recently, but I don't want to give up on us. I want to show you how much I love you every day. Watch out for more affection, more laughter." This can be a good start to getting things back on track.

Creating a Spark Without Touch

Not all foreplay is physical. There are many five-minute ways to add heat to your marriage without touching at all. In fact, when asked what most attracts them to their spouses, the majority of women (including Daisy) will say, "Oh, he makes me laugh." Not his hot body or full head of hair, and not his gigantic penis, but his ability to make her giggle. A sense of humor is one of the most powerful tools for keeping the spark alive. Laughter imbues your relationship with feelings of goodwill and happiness, and encourages you to be open emotionally and physically.

Paying attention to the visual is another way you can stimulate sexual thoughts. Keeping yourself attractive, if that is important to you and your partner, can stoke the flames of desire in even mundane moments. Perhaps he catches a quick glance at your décolletage as you bend down to pick up the mail. Or you love the way he appears in his suit as he heads off to a meeting. Though skin deep, your physical gifts can be used to remind each other of why you were initially attracted to the other way back when. If you feel that your appearance is important to you, but you have gained weight and lost confidence over the years, consider a personalized exercise program or a wardrobe update. Then be sure to notice when he stares at you from across the room.

SAY THIS

"I'm reading a great book on marriage that has a bunch of sexy tips. Don't be surprised if you find yourself unable to resist me!"

Take advantage of the world around you for arousal. Sex is everywhere—on the billboard you pass every day and in the movie you saw last night. When you pass a couple holding hands, kissing goodbye, cuddling on a park bench, or making out on a street corner, what is your reaction? Does it give you a warm feeling or do you think, "Ew, too mushy! Do they have to do this right in front of me?" Do you look away, or do you sneak a glance in order to share their good feelings for a moment? Stealing a glimpse at a happy couple is an inspiring five-minute action that can influence your environment. Nudge your husband or wife the next time you play voyeur, share that intimate moment, and put it to good use later.

Five-Minute Strategies

Devoting five minutes each day to enhancing the sexual atmosphere in your marriage has far-reaching implications. These seemingly small acts are actually reminders of your connection and mutual attraction, even if things have been a bit rocky of late. It's easy to slip out of the initial heat of your early relationship and into a marriage that feels more like a friendship than a love match, but these simple, daily, five-minute reminders of your attraction are a powerful way to keep you engaged with one another.

- Catch his eye over the dinner table and hold his gaze. Your meaningful glance will relay the message that more is on your mind than passing the green beans. That first spark you felt with your mate was probably through eye contact, and your shared gaze remains powerful.
- Create a private sign that means: "I want you." An ear tug or wink will mean nothing to those around you, but you'll both know what the other is thinking. Covert foreplay in public often adds to the sensual vibe you are seeking.
- Share an exciting visual, be it cinema, occasional pornography, or a salacious Calvin Klein ad with your partner. Is there a particular sex scene in your favorite movie that moves you whenever you see it? The next time it's on, call your partner into the room, and feel the charged atmosphere that appears.
- Tell yourself that your spouse is the only person on earth at this moment that can offer you sex. Your days are likely filled with responsibilities and compromises

that are decidedly un-sexy and sometimes, it can seem like you're running on parallel tracks with the person you married, just trying to get it all done. But, if you take a few minutes to think about your partner as your chosen lover, you'll feel more connected. This is foreplay's foreplay, getting yourself primed to reach out to your partner.

- Devise a language that only the two of you speak. Name your body parts so you can publicly say how you are looking forward to spending time with "Jorge" later on. This may seem silly, but sharing a laugh is actually a great way to engage in continuing foreplay. The connection you feel when you giggle together is one step away from the togetherness you share when you are intimate. In fact, laughing and togetherness often occur simultaneously.

- Predictability is not sexy. Surprise your spouse by introducing an arousing vibe into otherwise mundane moments. Ask him to take his shirt off while he's mowing the lawn. Give her a long, unbroken kiss while stopped at a red light. Sometimes it's the surprise that counts!

- Be mentally in synch. Finishing each other's sentences, being on the same page, agreeing on the route, the movie, the solution—all of these things give your relationship a flow that is sexy and at ease.

Chapter 4

Sexual Consciousness

Let's face it: Your day is packed with responsibilities both big and small. Who has time for sex when you have to get the kids out the door before the bus leaves? The challenge is to reprioritize sensuality so it's on par with your job, family, and chores. Research shows that sex is crucial to maintaining a stable, happy marriage—even though it may *seem* less urgent as the years go by. Indeed, a large study of over 15,000 adults entitled *Money, Sex and Happiness* showed a definite correlation between sexual activity and overall happiness. It keeps us young, connected, and vibrant, and colors an otherwise drab day with a rosy glow of contentment. The sexual connection you feel with your partner actually gives you the resilience to avoid petty arguments and resentments.

Of course, this book is dedicated to quick everyday solutions and, for many, a *satisfying* encounter is likely going to take longer than five minutes. But, by simply devoting even this small increment of time to sensuality, you will give your marriage every chance to thrive. In fact, a study published in the May 2008 issue of the *Journal of Sexual Medicine* surveyed thirty-four sex therapists who concluded that anywhere between three to thirteen minutes was optimal for pleasurable intercourse. So, no excuses!

Just Do It

Sex is a use-it-or-lose-it proposition. As time goes by, your love life begins to obey the law of inertia: Objects in motion stay in motion and objects at rest stay at rest. Engaging in sexual contact consistently over the course of a lifetime prevents a lack of desire from taking hold. You'll notice if there has been a hiatus in your sex life for health reasons or because life has simply been getting in the way, the anticipation of beginning anew may feel more like dread. The following list contains excuses or reasons for abstinence that are worth confronting. Once you let go, enjoy the moment, and surrender to the bliss of an encounter; nothing matches the pleasure you'll feel.

- **Laziness**: This is a matter of willing yourself to initiate sex instead of turning on the TV or computer. Don't count on your partner to take the lead. Instead, choose an opportune moment and get things started!
- **Busyness**: There's so much to do that by 10 P.M. you may be ready to pass out. Remind yourself that the benefits of sex far outweigh the minimal time it actually takes. Shouldn't reconnecting with your partner be at least as important as finishing up the dishes or that last bit of work you feel you need to get done?
- **Anger**: You hate his guts right now and unbelievably he's initiating sex. Actually, he has the right idea. Physical intimacy can smooth over a disagreement that you could have been brooding over for days.
- **Illness**: Often, a physical ailment takes sex completely off the table. Depending on the circumstance, using aids such as creams or Viagra or sporadic pornography

to assist in mutual masturbation can maintain vibrancy despite infirmity.

SAY THIS

"I know it's been a while, but I really miss you. Let's do whatever it takes to be intimate at least once a week."

ARLENE & ALAN'S STORY

Alan was the perfect fit for Arlene and her family. He was tall, went to the right schools, and was very ambitious. When she met him, Arlene was a virgin—a proper girl from a proper family. What she didn't know about Alan was that most of his sexual experiences were with professional sex workers. Arlene wanted to please Alan but was committed to wait until they were married to consummate the relationship. So Alan taught Arlene about blowjobs. Although it was very difficult for her, she accepted that it was what she needed to do to please her man.

Once they were married Alan had sex with Arlene every evening. He would climb on top of her, have an orgasm, roll off, and fall asleep. Arlene, who wasn't enjoying herself, believed there was something wrong with her. That is, until the day Pierre, her tennis instructor from the Bahamas, asked her if she would like to see his apartment. He had been describing his original art and wanted Arlene to give him her expert opinion on his work. That day began a torrid love affair that taught Arlene that she was a sexual person after all.

Her affair taught her that Alan was disconnected in the sexual arena and needed coaching to feel more comfortable letting her in. One day Arlene asked Alan to take a walk in the park so she could talk with him.

"Alan, I want to spice things up in the bedroom and add stimulation so I am more likely to orgasm."

"What? Are you saying that I'm not good in bed?"

"Alan, I don't want you to think that you are not a good lover, but by working together we can become a sexier team. I want to work on both of us feeling more comfortable together in bed."

"What's the problem? I am comfortable in bed with you."

"I need more time to become aroused."

"Um, okay. How?"

Arlene paused. She had never spoken in such an explicit way. "I need you to have oral sex with me. That would turn me on."

"Done. Works for me!"

The evolution of Arlene and Alan's sex life took more than one five-minute conversation. But Arlene left the park resolved to break it off with Pierre and throw herself wholeheartedly into making her marital bed more satisfying. She felt guilty about violating her marriage vows, grateful that Alan never discovered this breach, and hopeful that she could repair and improve the relationship now that she had more of an idea of her own sexual identity.

If you feel that you have sexual needs that are not being met, it's important to help your spouse find a way to please you. If you keep your need to expand your sexual repertoire hidden, you risk resentment bubbling over into other areas of your life. Although you may feel shy, embarrassed, or demanding, suggesting how to broaden the bedroom experience is a sign of sexual maturity.

SAY THIS

"I love what we do in bed. And I have some new ideas of how we can make things even more fun. Are you open to trying something fresh?"

Everyday Benefits

Sex can be difficult; we are literally naked, vulnerable in our desire. But keep in mind that the act offers a range of perks that can have a real, lasting effect on quality of life. Sex is entertainment. It is fun, enjoyable, and gratifying. You can laugh, giggle, have private jokes, or even a private language. Sometimes it is much easier to bring the computer or baby into bed in order to avoid our partners, but five minutes a day for a sexy encounter adds fun to daily life.

Extra Credit

Sex in a semi-public place—such as the beach at night, the golf course after hours, or your own back yard or kitchen—demands brevity. And the risk of being caught may intensify your gratification.

Not only is sex pleasurable, having it often means you don't have to feel guilty about skipping the gym now and again. It is a major calorie-burner and, just like all exercise, the advantages range from a trimmer waistline to a better night's sleep. And the health benefits don't stop there. For men, sex keeps the prostate gland vibrant and in use and a study in the *British Medical Journal* shows that the mortality rate is 50 percent lower for men who have frequent orgasms over men who don't. For women, sex maintains a hormonal balance. Both genders experience less stress and depression, plus better immunity when their sex lives are active. Some studies go so far as to hold that sex may reduce the risk of the two leading causes of death in the United States: heart disease and cancer.

Extra Credit

Throughout the day, fantasize about your next encounter. Daydream when you drive, when you feed the baby, and when you make dinner. By the time you meet your partner in bed, you'll be primed and ready.

Sex is a form of nonverbal communication that demonstrates that you care about your partner. This is a strong draw for people who are uncomfortable using words. Among this group is a substantial cohort of people who love expressing themselves through their bodies. They find it the most relaxing, undemanding, freeing part of their lives. In contrast, speaking from the heart is a more tedious challenge. That said, having sex often encourages reticent lovers to verbally speak their vulnerable feelings. Hormones such as oxytocin (often referred to as the "cuddle hormone") that are released during orgasm will help you feel less inhibited and closer to your partner, which encourages mutual bonding.

We all wear many hats in our lives: From mommy or daddy to manager, your roles are ever-shifting. Make being a lover a key life role. After all, you're much more than a mom with baby food on her sleeve, or a dad battling a never-ending to-do list. For a few minutes a day, embrace a role that is juicy and exciting or mysterious and bold. Let your inner lover shine through and you'll capture your partner's attention as well as all the benefits of a vibrant sex life.

Five-Minute Strategies

Given our busy lives, everyday intercourse is often brief by necessity. Rather than bemoaning this fact, embrace it and commit to making sex a priority in your marriage. Like exercise and eating right, think of it as a preventative measure that keeps your relationship healthy and strong. Anyone can carve out five minutes to be intimate, so be creative and discover the many emotional and physical benefits of a satisfying sex life.

- Be open about what you enjoy about your current sex life—and what you feel may be missing. A brief conversation conducted with humor and love will give each of you the opportunity to honestly propose new ideas. If you're too shy to talk about sex directly, give your spouse hints as to what you desire the next time you make love. A well-timed moan or touch may speak volumes, depending on the other person's capacity to read between the lines.
- Enjoy a "quickie" before the kids wake up or during a lunch break. The research shows sex doesn't have to last hours to be satisfying. The rosy glow that a sexy twosome provides far outweighs a five-minute snooze or work session.
- Hop into your mate's morning shower for a few sensual minutes. The combination of warm water and cleansing lubricants could be irresistible. And, don't underestimate the power of shaking up your routine. The shower is just one variation on the bed that can heat up your standard repertoire. Consider the spare

room, kitchen, or den (when you're assured your kids and neighbors are unlikely to interrupt!).

- Having a bad day? In a fight with your spouse? Getting busy may be the last thing on your mind, but I challenge you to witness the transformative power of sex. Making love even during the tough times can shore up a rocky period in your life or in your relationship. Work through your resistance and keep in mind that much can be made up for in the bedroom.

- Give the gift of oral sex without an expectation of reciprocation. This generous act will be mutually gratifying when you see your spouse go through the day mellow and relaxed.

- Join your spouse in bed in just a thong or a T-shirt with nothing underneath. No need for frilly nightwear, which many people find too over the top. You may be more comfortable in subtle, cozy cotton than unyielding leather and itchy lace. Sometimes sexy is simple. On the other hand, if dressing up turns you or your partner on, by all means go for it. Nothing ventured, nothing gained.

- Whisper a flirty message in your lover's ear when you pass her in the hall, asking her to meet you in private. Then lock the door and enjoy! As we discussed in the previous chapter, infusing daily life with surprising foreplay will prime you for a happy sexual encounter.

- Commit to going to bed at the same time (and keep the television off!). Opportunity is key to keeping sex alive in your marriage. If one of you is more of a night owl than the other, that person can always go back to her television, book, or computer after you've made love.

Chapter 5

Fight Resistance, Keep the Connection Alive

We all have moments when we would rather not be physical: We're too tired, too sweaty, too stressed. However, *consistently* resisting your partner's initiation can be deadening. Ideally, when affection is offered—he pulls you in close for a hug, she asks how you are feeling about work these days—you wholeheartedly surrender to the moment. By hugging him back or opening up about your stress level, you close the circle with reciprocation and keep the connection alive.

Why Snub Love?

Resistance to your spouse's offer of sex or any other form of affection can be the result of shyness, fear, shame, or habit. Most often, it is rooted in childhood experiences that still influence your life. Because we are often unaware of how the past is affecting the present, resistance can be difficult to stamp out. The more insight you gain about the experiences that have fed this unintentional barricade, the less it will control you. No need to be alarmed: There are five-minute, daily strategies that can help you overcome your habitual opposition and embrace your spouse's offerings.

Do the following situations sound familiar? Perhaps you have allowed resistance to dampen your light.

- You've just sat down and turned on the television to watch a favorite program. Your spouse happily plops beside you and snuggles up. Feeling crowded, you get up to grab a soda and then settle back in a different chair.
- Heading out the door, your husband goes in for a kiss on the lips. You quickly turn your head and offer him your cheek, not wanting to smear your lipstick.
- It's been a month since you and your partner have had sex, but you feel heavy these days. He comes to bed earlier than usual and kisses the back of your neck. You pretend you're already dreaming.
- For the third night in a row, your toddler begs to sleep in your bed. You give in, ignoring your partner's pleas for privacy, ensuring an intimacy-free evening.
- On the long car ride home after visiting your aging parents, your husband asks you probing questions about how you are handling the painful truth of your parents' decline. Your response, a rhetorical: "How do you think I feel?"

Rejecting your partner's outreach is, over time, a precarious endeavor. The lack of sexual and emotional reciprocation is one of the primary reasons dissatisfied people seek comfort outside of their marriages. A 2008 study in the *Journal of Sex and Medicine* concludes: "Dissatisfaction with the intimacy in the primary relationship was directly related to motivations for extra dyadic involvement focused on meeting unmet intimacy needs." It becomes easier for the partner who feels rejected to have an affair or to hide in the basement with online porn than to keep beating down the door of your resistance. Avoid such a drastic scenario by combating your opposition, bit by bit, each day.

Breaking Shame's Spell

As much as we say we want to be happy, it can be difficult to make our hearts do what our heads will not. Sidestepping an offer of intimacy is often rooted in shame. You may think, "If we make love he'll surely notice my fat thighs and stomach. It's better to avoid sex altogether." Or, "I have nothing interesting to say. I don't deserve to be listened to." These negative messages are love inhibitors. Your partner may walk away stung by your rejection, not realizing that it has nothing to do with him, and everything to do with the discomfort you've been lugging around your whole life because your mom called you "big-boned" or because you had a distant dad. It's time to strip shame of its power by exposing it to the light.

MARTIN & AVA'S STORY

After twenty-five years of marriage and countless attempts, Ava had reached out for her husband, Martin, only to have him roll further to his side of the bed. In fact, in the last five years they had sex less than a dozen times. And those rare events usually occurred after Martin came home from a business meeting where things went well. He had shared good wine and would approach Ava from behind while she was deeply asleep.

Only Martin's best friend, Jack, who knew him as a boy and understood that he was not the favorite child, had compassion for Martin's self-inflicted deprivation when it came to sleeping with Ava. Over beers one night, Jack reminded Martin that he was the child who never got new clothes, only the hand-me-downs from his two older brothers. He was the kid who had to watch all of the baseball games that his jock brothers played week after week. His father and mother cheered wholeheartedly for the big boys and had little interest in Martin's passion for tennis.

SAY THIS

"I know we haven't had a chance to connect (verbally/physically) lately, and I miss you. Let's sit down for a brief moment with our calendars and make a date."

What could Martin say to Ava to explain the connection between his childhood sadness and their paltry sex life? After his illuminating conversation with Jack, Martin started to mend the situation with Ava by saying, "I've been thinking about our sex life. We need to do it more."

"Wow, where did this come from?"

"I was speaking to Jack the other day and he reminded me of what happened to me as a child. I've told you that I was basically ignored growing up."

"Yes, but what does this have to do with sex?"

"I see now that I am used to being deprived and that I do it now when I'm in bed with you. Do you want to work on getting things hot and steamy again?"

"Count me in! When do we start?"

"Let's make Friday evening our night to reconnect."

Martin was open to feedback from Jack, and was able to link the past to the present. By Ava and Martin agreeing to a set time there was little room to wiggle out of the new direction they were taking as a couple.

Close your own loopholes. Be proactive in your marriage by scheduling a time to combat your usual resistance. If you tend to clam up, carve out a time to talk. If you avoid sex, put a "sex night" on the calendar.

Use Your Insight

Discovering why you resist your partner's offerings of emotional connection may take time, and could involve therapy or long talks with a good friend. But once you have a keen understanding of what makes you tick, it only takes a few minutes a day to focus on eradicating negative patterns of behavior.

Extra Credit

Why wait for your partner to make the first move? The ultimate way to fight your resistance is to take a deep breath and seize your destiny. Even if it's uncomfortable, initiate intimacy and your doubts will soon seem less controlling.

One strategy is to set aside five minutes a day to meditate. Often the best time to do this is first thing in the morning. Before you even get out of bed, sit up, stretch, and engage in deep breathing exercises. Allow your body and mind to gently greet the day. If negative thoughts intrude, acknowledge them and remind yourself that you are not a helpless victim of your past. Focus on cultivating loving-kindness to yourself. As you become more proficient in this you will naturally offer it to your spouse.

A variation is to notice your negative mantras and turn them into positive statements. The more you put something that humiliates you into words, the more you are able to overcome it. Changing your dark tune into a light one is a valuable daily exercise that takes little time, but has a lasting effect. Notice if your self-talk becomes negative and replace weakening thoughts with an empowering mantra. See the following chart for some ideas on how to change your mantra in just five minutes a day.

Shame Mantra	Love-Myself Mantra
I don't deserve happiness.	Happiness is a universal right, and one I am committed to embracing.
I'm fat.	I am beautiful no matter what size I am.
Why would anyone want to listen to me?	My ideas and feelings are unique and interesting.
A loving relationship is what other people have, not us.	I am committed to doing everything possible to enhance my marriage.
He/she can't really love me.	I deserve love and he/she is lucky to have me.

Over time, not being "in the mood" or snubbing your spouse's attempts at closeness will erode a happy union. The beauty of breaking through your out-of-the-gate resistance, however, is that your feelings will often shift from grumpy and cautious to "Hey, this actually feels really good!" Take a leap of faith and overcome your hesitation. In these few minutes, you'll shore up your chances for long-term happiness. The more you act as if you are secure in receiving his affectionate attachment, the more you will change the structure of your brain to actually crave the warmth of a secure attachment.

Five-Minute Strategies

Resisting your partner's offers of physical or emotional affection can become habitual. Over time, your spouse may stop trying to reach out to you. The good news: It only takes five minutes a day to vanquish shame's tentacles and happily accept the love that is being offered.

- For a few minutes a day write your thoughts and feelings in a journal in order to make yourself conscious of your tendency toward resistance. What's at the root of your desire to push your partner to the sidelines? Focusing on this is the first step to overcoming it.
- Notice those instances when your partner is stung by you being too tired or uncommunicative. In those moments there is an opportunity to repair the damage by reaching out and reassuring her with words of love or a promise to reschedule. Be careful: Too many rejections may send your partner to seek solace outside of your relationship.
- Take a fresh look at your childhood experiences. Is there anything from your past that still haunts you, causing you to feel that you don't deserve your partner's offerings of love? Most of our feelings of shame are rooted in our earliest experiences. Acknowledging what occurred in the past is the first step toward moving beyond it.
- Change your negative mantra to a positive one. We are all so hard on ourselves. Whenever you hear your brain sending its usual unconstructive messages, hit your mental delete button and replace them with positive

thoughts. Be disciplined! It may take time to vanquish these mental devils, but with daily practice, you will.

- Call a trusted friend or counselor and schedule a time for a heart-to-heart talk. Often, talking to someone outside your marriage can reveal hidden truths that you may not have found on your own. Describe a specific instance when you passed up on your spouse's offer of affection and see what a new point of view can teach you about that event.

- Schedule a specific time to connect with your spouse. Putting a date night on the calendar when you both expect to bond emotionally and physically will combat any excuses you may have. You can prepare yourself to be open and willing to engage by applying the advice from this chapter. Then, enjoy the time spent with this person with whom you chose to spend your life. See her wonderful qualities.

- Engage even if you feel momentarily uncomfortable. Initiate lovemaking or an intimate conversation where you express yourself authentically. Once you feel that unmistakable connection take hold, your initial discomfort is unlikely to last.

Chapter 6

Embrace the New

Inevitably, most marriages settle into a routine. You may not remember why you always sleep on the right side of the bed or why Tuesday night is taco night. It just is. And predictability—especially if you grew up in a chaotic environment—can be a comfort. But studies show that couples who refresh, surprise, and explore together remain happier than those who don't.

Embracing experiences such as traveling to an unfamiliar city, or simply choosing a new restaurant, enhance togetherness. When you venture into uncharted territory as a team, you take a risk and have a story to tell. Your partner seems more attractive. And the memory of your shared adventure burns brighter than the hundreds of nights you predictably sat down in front of the television or frequented your usual Saturday night date spot.

Conflict over Change

Although research supports the power of newness, it may be that you are more comfortable with change than your spouse, or vice versa. Being the one to initiate novelty is stimulating but can also be destabilizing. Frequent quarrels take place over one person wanting, for example, to spontaneously invite friends over, or to go out to the theater or to a new restaurant. The other spouse may become annoyed. She may say: "You are never satisfied. You are always changing things." or, "Am I not good enough for you? I just want some peace and quiet in my home." A perennial struggle between spouses occurs: Just when they finally settle on a good restaurant, he wants to try the Ethiopian place down the street, or just when she gets into a television series, he becomes bored and wants to change the channel.

> ### *Extra Credit*
> What are some five-minute strategies that can infuse your marriage with adventure? The possibilities are endless. Grab pen and paper and write down your daily routine. Then, for each predictable action, choose something surprising.

How frustrating and how marvelous! The person who loves variety will be appreciated if he is sensitive to his partner's discomfort at leaving the familiar. Reticence toward change reflects a need for control and is often connected to finding risk taking destabilizing. Predictability provides stability that real life does not. It is kind to go along with the routine and it is courageous to want to change what is working, but couple transformations are ultimately what keep a pair engaged and not looking elsewhere for escapades.

MARCY & ROBERT'S STORY

Robert never got a passport, and his wife Marcy loved to travel. Last year at a cooking school in Tuscany she hiked each day after class with a man from Dallas.

When she returned she told Robert about the entire trip, including the hiking adventure. He blew his stack, yelling, "How dare you?" He then went into the bedroom, locked the door and threw things around for over a half an hour. Marcy banged on the door for him to let her in, but he refused. She was horrified.

The next day they decided to go to the local diner for breakfast and talk. This time Robert began and Marcy chose to hear him out.

"Does this guy from Dallas look better than me or speak about more interesting things than I do? Just because he likes to travel and I hate it, does that mean he has rights to my wife?"

"Robert, why do you think this guy had his way with me?"

"Because I know you very well. You can be gullible, and if Mr. Dallas said the right things to you, you could easily be duped. After all, I know what I said to get you to marry me."

"What?"

"You are the most beautiful woman in the world to me, the smartest, the funniest, the kindest."

"Do you still feel that way about me?"

"Yes."

"Well then, I'm still gullible because I love you very much also. But living our whole life in Kansas City and never traveling is just too confining for me. Would you consider taking a fear of flying course offered by the airlines?"

"Yes, but don't count on me to ever fly."

"Well at least now I know that you're willing to try something new."

With this five-minute conversation, Robert saw the handwriting on the wall. Marcy was not a woman you could confine. He loved his home and his life but realized if he never confronted his fear of flying he ran the risk that next time it could be more than just hiking. Marcy's willingness to go to the diner with him and hear out his side of the conflict gave him confidence that he had not already lost her. It spurred him on to try to confront his fear of flying.

The Risk of Routine

Routine can be deadening if one spouse's tolerance for change exceeds the other's. Without compromise, the risk-loving partner will seek new experiences alone. At best, this will lead to a feeling of disconnect as the spouse who stays home feels left out of new friendships, travel opportunities, or other novel experiences, and the one who ventures out feels as if he is always on his own. At worst, this mismatch can lead to a mate succumbing to infidelity. New people may seem infinitely more interesting than the same old, same old who wants dinner at 7 P.M. followed by a walk around the block.

Inflexibility is an impediment to a contented atmosphere in a long-term marriage. Conversely, compulsively searching for the new restaurant, outfit, or vacation spot could imply that what is at home can never measure up. This could also lead to a partner feeling defeated or looking elsewhere for appreciation.

To counter these risks, the first step is to appreciate your or your spouse's resistance to change. It doesn't take long in a partnership to see which of you tends to push new experiences and which of you opposes. (Quick test: Who is more likely to say, "Aw, let's just stay in tonight"?) If you approach change with ease, take five minutes a day to encourage your mate to take baby steps out of his comfort zone. This could mean creating a vegetarian meal for your meat-loving man, or putting on music that challenges her light-rock ear. Stay positive and avoid judgmental statements that might make your more-cautious partner feel boring or like a scaredy-cat.

SAY THIS

"Let's shake things up a bit tonight. You take your pick: We can try the new sushi place in town or invite our neighbors over for a drink."

If you tend to avoid change, take these incremental steps with your more adventurous spouse; go with the flow while maintaining your integrity. Embracing discomfort can prevent your partner from feeling isolated. Imagine, for example, your spouse approaches you with blueprints to put a new addition on the house. Your initial reaction may be to refuse, claiming the house is fine the way it is or there's not enough money. Consider a different approach by saying something like, "Honey, thanks for taking this initiative. I would feel more comfortable starting this home improvement project on a smaller scale. Haven't you always wanted to redo the master bath?"

Taking small steps toward modification may encourage you to eventually embrace larger challenges—a trip, perhaps, or a new job or friendship. After all, life is change. By resisting this fact and transforming your home life into a falsely static environment, you or your partner are denying yourselves the pleasure of the new.

Five-Minute Strategies

Help your partner (or yourself) to take five-minute endeavors toward novelty and protect your marriage from the dead end of predictability. For those who embrace comfort and control, introducing change in such small increments can bring newness into your life without rocking the boat. The possibilities for change are endless. Be creative and invite newness into your culinary life, your sex life, your social life, and your travels.

- Rather than sleeping as late as possible and then rushing through your morning in order to not be late, wake up five minutes early and make breakfast or initiate weekday sex. Think of these five minutes as bonus minutes, to fill with anything you like—as long as what you choose is out of your usual routine.
- When running errands with your spouse, choose a scenic route and stop off at a pretty overlook or park for a few minutes. This will create a memorable experience that taking your usual route through town would not. Your partner may look at you funny when you deviate from your usual drive. Smile and say you wanted to take a moment together in a setting as beautiful as she.
- It's movie night! Resist renting the latest blockbuster. Instead, go with the indie flick the kid at the counter swears by. Embracing change can even mean going outside your comfort zones in terms of art and entertainment. In our thriving culture, there is always something new to discover—a new band that's playing downtown or an exhibit by an up-and-coming artist. Challenge

your assumptions. You don't have to be a convert to the latest thing, but the experience may open your eyes.

- After returning home from work, you may be tempted to change into your usual comfy pair of yoga pants; instead, don a pretty sundress or bottom-hugging pair of jeans. Staying in tonight? Put on your sexy new underwear for your partner to eventually discover. This is not a suggestion that you spend your relaxation hours in high heels and skin-tight leather, but putting aside your standard duds may spark some interest.

- The usual scene: After dinner you read your novel and he reads his paper. Instead, choose a book or magazine that you are both interested in and read it simultaneously. Then watch the conversational sparks fly as you discuss the plot or premise. You could also choose a card or board game you both enjoy and add it to your evening repertoire.

- Challenge your palate—and your culinary skills—and choose one night a week to plan something new for dinner. Look through the multitude of online recipes for, perhaps, a vegetarian entrée, or something exotic like a Moroccan-inspired tangine.

- Your usual moves in bed are tried and true—and tired. Peruse the *Kama Sutra* and pick a pose that you and your partner can try. Alternate weeks; one week you choose an exciting new position, the next week your spouse decides. This gives you both some control over the direction of your sex life.

PART 2

Five-Minute Strategies for Domestic Bliss

Chapter 7

Make the Mundane
Meaningful

Everyday life can wreak havoc on a marriage and an uneven delegation of housework is a primary cause of stress. Over the past forty years women have taken their place in the workforce, yet the majority of housework still falls on female shoulders. In fact, a study out of Brown University entitled *Gender, Household Labor, and Psychological Distress: The Impact of the Amount and Division of Housework* maintains that, among married couples, women perform over 70 percent of the household labor. This discrepancy contributes greatly to gender differences in physiological well-being. In addition, the so-called "second shift" often ensures that there is little time for couple togetherness after the workday. Dinner, dishes, and laundry often take precedence over conversation, sex, or relaxation.

Many women who come into my office *want* to be in charge of the kids' schedule, bake the cupcakes for school, and know the family budget inside and out. This desire for control rewards them with a sense of accomplishment and security, but it doesn't forestall the resentment that she feels toward her husband when he is standing on the sidelines watching everything run smoothly, but doing little to help. Often from his viewpoint, he is giving space for autonomy, and avoiding crowding his spouse.

The challenge of maintaining a balanced marriage within these parameters can seem daunting. Fortunately, with minimal daily effort, many bumps in the road to happiness can be avoided.

A Little Means a Lot

A certain outlook for the division of labor exists within every marriage. If both partners aren't happy with the level of expectation, one partner or both may feel that the other isn't holding up his end of the bargain, which builds antipathy. Happily, with effort you can balance the scales. Many chores take less than five minutes, and earn hours of appreciation. Putting the dishes in the dishwasher or taking out the garbage may seem trivial, but demonstrate a couple working together generously.

SAY THIS

"I realize that having a clean and neat environment is more important to me than it is to you, but I'd appreciate you lending a hand. You spend the most time in the den (garage/kitchen/bedroom), so maybe that room can be your responsibility? What do you think?"

These types of tasks may seem obvious. Of course, it's not *difficult* to make the bed. So, why doesn't every marriage sail along smoothly with her doing 50 percent and him matching her task-for-task? Many people come to my office complaining that their spouse just doesn't *see* the dirty floor or sink full of dishes. This could be because, growing up, there wasn't housework training. Or, perhaps your partner has a higher tolerance for disorder than you do. The challenge in this case is to find and delegate the tasks he is most likely to deem essential. He may never notice the laundry, happily wearing the same pair of boxers day in and day out. Rather than fight that losing battle, what does he have a stake in? Organizing the mud room? Vacuuming the den? Mowing the lawn?

LAUREN & BOB'S STORY

Lauren is drowning in bitterness toward her husband, Bob. One Sunday the whole family went to a street fair together where many of the people in their community said hello to Lauren, Bob, and their children. Within a very short time Bob was standing on the sidelines smoking a cigarette. Lauren was furious. Rather than joining her and the children and saying hello to teachers, doctors, and friends, Bob leaned against the wall as if he was not also responsible for making the children feel comfortable in the community.

"Bob, put away that cigarette!" she shouted.

He yelled back: "You can't tell me what to do!"

Later, as she struggled to put both children into the double stroller, Bob stood and watched. He showed no indication that he was also one of the children's parents. Lauren was furious again. At home she cooked, and fed, and played with the kids 24/7. Bob worked hard at his job as a recruiter and then came home and disappeared into the TV room to play video games. As much as she loved him sometimes she felt like she was his mother and she hated it. He hated it even more.

During dinner that night Lauren asked, "What happened at the street fair?"

Bob's response: "You sounded like my uptight mother. We're a team and you were speaking to me like I was a bad schoolboy."

"I understand that my voice sounded like an angry mother. And the fact is, I am one! I don't want to be on your case and not on your team, but from my point of view, I needed you to help with the kids and you were off smoking."

Lauren is aware that Bob's mom is uptight and angry and she knows that he reflexively rebels when he hears that tone in her voice. At the same time, Lauren also grew up with some unpleasant family memories. When she was a child it was just her and her mom. Her mother took custody of Lauren and her father did not fight for time with her. Now, when Bob does not participate with her and the children those feelings of abandonment are triggered.

"Bob, I love that you feel we're a team. Let's choose a time to sit down and hash out exactly what that means so we are both happy."

"I agree. I'm off on Saturday. Let's have your mom watch the kids while we go down to the lake."

By choosing a time away from the stress of the kids and home, Bob and Lauren set the stage for a successful dialogue. Ideally, they would agree to share more of the domestic duties, while still allowing Bob to come home and decompress after work. The theme is respecting each others' space as well as finding good couple time to speak, keeping in mind that each partner has a personal history and agreeing to be sensitive to it so that past pain is minimized in the present.

The Power of the Unexpected

Appreciation for your spouse tends to be heightened by the unexpected. Take a few minutes to imagine what domestic duty you could complete that would make him smile. You don't have to mop the floor. You can get creative by asking your partner if she would mind if you try rearranging the furniture in a more pleasing way or finally framing and hanging your vacation photos. Little touches like this make a house a home, a haven from the stress of the outside world.

Extra Credit

Call your in-laws. Few gestures are more appreciated than tackling the weekly (or monthly) check-in. Sure, you do it with your parents, but what a treat—for your spouse and for them—to take it upon yourself to tell your mother- or father-in-law all the latest news.

Also consider that, in many households, the work is divvied up along gender lines. This can make already tiresome jobs feel even more thankless. Take five minutes to surprise him by doing one of his jobs. If he cooks, you plan the meal. If she vacuums, you tackle the rugs. The surprise element will make these tasks count even more.

Everyday life is made up of the mundane, but with appreciation of the miracle of being alive, together, and having the basics, the ordinary becomes holy. The fabric of daily living, when done with a sense of purpose, can elevate you to a feeling that your life is worthwhile, and that you're helping to make someone else's life worth living as well.

Five-Minute Strategies

Tackling everyday tasks is really just a matter of paying attention. Taking out the garbage or feeding the pets are not taxing jobs. That said, most of us would rather ignore or sidestep what needs to be done, and spend those five minutes with our feet up. But these tasks are more than they seem. Accomplishing them means you are thoughtful and generous, qualities every spouse deems admirable. Chores also mean that you respect your environment and the other people that live in it. There are limitless possibilities for making the mundane meaningful in five minutes a day. Here are some starters:

- Set the table before dinner, complete with folded napkins and drinks. Not having to do this job will make the cook feel appreciated and avoid the usual getting-the-food-on-the-table frenzy.
- Make a calendar for your household, delegating who is responsible for what and on which days. Having it written down can avoid arguments about who does what, especially if you have children who resist chipping in.
- Sweep the floor while you are on the phone or watching a ball game. Watch the baby while you wash dishes. Walk the dog while you brainstorm about a work project. Multitasking during these mindless chores will make it feel as though the household is under better control.
- Take the kids for a ride around the block when they are getting out of control. A change in environment can help contain the chaos. And, the peace of a quiet

house for a few minutes will lower your spouse's blood pressure.

- Get up a few minutes early and make the morning coffee/tea. What a treat for the rest of the household to wander (or rush) downstairs to caffeine at the ready.
- Bring in the paper, no matter how inclement the weather. This allows your loved one to stay in her slippers for a few minutes longer in the morning. Remember to grab the mail on your way in or out of the house.
- One duty that takes little time and that everyone resists is cleaning the toilet. Caring for this weekly task shows your partner that you are willing to take one for the team.
- Ask your spouse what chore he particularly dreads. Then promise to take it on yourself, no matter how unpleasant.
- Keep up with the bills. It only requires a few minutes to write the checks, or, better yet, sign up for automatic bill pay. Financial stress in your home will ease knowing the gas, phone, and water bills are covered.
- Every once in a while, when finances allow, call a cleaning service to deep clean your house. This will be money well spent, as your household will feel the relief of undone chores vanishing into air. The sight of dust-free baseboards and sparkling windows will make you smile, and not having to dust and wipe gives you more quality time with your honey.

Chapter 8

Big Gestures

The big gestures that are sprinkled throughout a marriage—honeymoon, milestones, birthdays, significant anniversaries, vow renewals, lifecycle celebrations, adventure trips—are as important as sharing in the everyday. These special times infuse your relationship with excitement, happy anticipation, and fond memories that can sustain you through your more difficult periods.

So, for example, you can always go to your usual mid-price Italian restaurant for her birthday. But wouldn't a picnic at a local winery be more memorable? As we discussed in Chapter 6, inviting novelty into your marriage is an important way to keep the relationship vibrant. It supports the desire to feel the fire, a verve to please your partner, to want to experience something unique and meaningful together.

Looking Forward

Planning a big event or trip engages ingenuity, and the journey is often as important as the destination. Researching spas, discussing side trips, and anticipating the vacation confers togetherness even before you get on the plane! Surprising your partner with an anniversary gift or party imbues your marriage with a spark as you consider what piece of jewelry she would like best, or which DJ he would find most entertaining at the party. Planning a surprise keeps your partner in the forefront of your mind and adds to the warmth between you, even if your spouse isn't exactly sure why you are being so thoughtful. Together or separate, anticipation is a significant addition to the joy of a big gesture.

Of course, planning an event, trip, or gift often takes a large amount of time. So, how can you view the big gestures through the framework of five minutes? Anticipation means dreaming about how wonderful the party is going to be as you go about your day handling a difficult client, soothing cranky children, or walking the dog in the pouring rain. It's the expectation of warm sand between your toes while you walk to the subway in February's cold blast. Looking forward to an event or trip can bring at least half the pleasure. For a few minutes each day, think about the carefree time you are about to spend with your spouse, or the way her eyes will shine when she sees you've arranged for all her closest girlfriends to be at her birthday. Talk about your excitement for the upcoming anniversary for a few minutes over dinner or in the car. The joyful discussions are also a sharing experience.

Looking Back

Harvard scientist Dr. Daniel Gilbert reports, "Married people are happier than unmarried ones, perhaps because the single best predictor of human happiness is the quality of social relationships. Marriage seems to buy you a decade or more of longevity." People are happiest when they're having sex and talking, or otherwise investing in social relationships. Resting and relaxing doesn't guarantee happiness because when you're not engaged in a task—even a generally unpleasant one—your mind can wander, and you may ruminate on unhappy experiences.

Extra Credit

Take a Sunday afternoon and look through your old photos. Pick one that you feel evokes a happy time—a trip or wedding or other special occasion. Then, surprise your spouse by e-mailing it to her at work or placing it on the fridge for her to find.

This builds the case for planning happy events. It fills your thoughts with hope beforehand and warm memories following the experience. Recalling a trip you took together can flood you with joy, even if you don't have any money or time to leave home base at this moment. One couple I know quit their jobs two years after marriage and took a trip around the world. They each had a very large backpack and that was that. Staying in youth hostels, hiking in Nepal, biking in Italy, and walking the boulevards of Buenos Aires, were an exhilarating, adventurous experience. Now, a decade later, these jetsetters have full-time jobs, and juggle a multitude of activities for their three young children, the baby sitters, and their family, and have minimal alone time. Thankfully, this trip sustains them beyond what they could have imagined while planning or executing it.

Use the memory of the gift your spouse gave you all those years ago, or the couples massage you shared in a candle-lit Mexican cave, to infuse your current reality with pleasure or romance. Remembering your life experiences will buoy you up during more down-to-earth times. When things are looking dreary (car trouble, teething baby, burned dinner), remind your partner of a pleasurable memory the two of you have shared.

SAY THIS

"Things are hard right now, but remember how wonderful our wedding day was? I was so in love with you then, but I couldn't imagine how the challenges we've faced since have made me love you even more."

Big Gestures for the Wrong Reasons

Sadly, a disclaimer is in order. It is not uncommon for spouses who are abusive to use major events, gifts, or generous acts in an attempt to distract their partner from their abusive behavior. They may erroneously try to cover over the destructive parts of the relationship. If you find your partner makes amends for damage in everyday life through overly demonstrative gestures, please know that there is no substitute for safety in a relationship, for respect in all of the small ways—such as walking the dog, changing the diapers, bountiful hugs, doing the dishes, or giving a compliment in the course of everyday life. Asking an assistant to send an extravagant anniversary gift and then spending the day with a secret lover is the ultimate undoing and degrading of a long-term love. Each partner must resist this behavior. After all, trying to pay off a wrong by making some big gestures is morally corrupt.

Authenticity counts above all else. If the big gesture truly represents the emotional wish to find passion, support, comfort, and safety within the marriage, these events bolster this goal. If the large ring, two dozen roses, or plane tickets are meant to assuage guilt, quiet the disgruntled, or leave space for recurring disrespect or even abuse, then the generosity of the moment is hollow.

The Importance of Community

Big moments in our marriages often involve the surrounding community, and for good reason. A marriage that is supported by loved ones tends to maintain its strength if it has a reliable foundation of friends and family. Lifecycle events, such as christenings, bat and bar mitzvahs, and vow renewals are celebrations of these bonds. And, in a culture where families tend to disperse, these events bring us together.

In my own practice and in the lives of my friends and relatives I have experienced many lifecycle events that reinforce community and assure all concerned of how much love and support are available when and if the need arises. Our commitment to our spouses and family spreads a canopy of warmth over all the others in our larger circle. The more big gestures we invest in, the more opportunities we have to celebrate that love.

NANCY & LAURENT'S STORY

Nancy and Laurent eloped twenty years ago, not out of choice but because neither partner believed that anyone in their community approved of their marriage. Nancy came from a blue-collar family and Laurent was a blue-blood WASP. Nancy's mother worked at the post office for thirty years and her dad worked on the railroad. Laurent's father was an admiral in the navy and raised his children with the disciplinary strictness that he imparted to staff. Laurent had felt unprotected by his mother and was under critical observation by his father. Bereft of support, unable to please his father, he could not imagine walking down the aisle as a bridegroom with all of the faces of his family oozing disapproval.

Laurent needed the continuing shoring up and comfort from his calm, adoring wife and her nondemanding parents and relatives. He began to meditate on a daily basis in order to develop a consciousness of loving kindness toward himself. After living as husband and wife for over two decades, including having four children, they discussed having a ceremony to renew their marriage vows.

"I don't know, Laurent. Having what amounts to another wedding may bring up all the pain of our early years. Your parents haven't made much of an effort to be involved in our lives."

"Yes, but we'll be doing it for us, not for them. And, I feel like it's an act of forgiveness to include them in our happiness."

"Okay, I'll go along with it, but I have my doubts."

It turns out that Laurent was right. The day turned out to be a near-perfect experience. Nancy and Laurent felt the approval from all of their parents and other relatives and their folks bonded during the occasion. The photographer captured it all, and Nancy and Laurent sent these photos to friends around the world to share in their joy.

From a neurobiological point of view, both Nancy and Laurent were able to reshape the structure of their brains. In adulthood when we feel understood, early childhood memories (called implicit memories) of feeling that there was no one to depend on can be reworked and changed. A brain scan can actually physically document these changes. On a behavioral level, when we feel as though we are seen and understood for who we are, we become able to respond to others in a more secure, relaxed manner rather than responding from a place of insecurity. This is what happened for Laurent. At the renewal of vows ceremony, both of his parents were beaming with approval, and it helped him feel as if he had finally become an acceptable member of society in his father's eyes and therefore in his own eyes as well. When this happened the earlier implicit memories (Laurent's maternal safety deficit and the feeling that he wasn't good enough for his father) became available for incorporation in the developing narrative of his life. He could now file these memories away; they were no longer toxic to his present life.

Nancy and Laurent's big day was wonderful for their marital bond as well. They enjoyed every aspect of the planning, and savored the memory of their perfect vow renewal celebration for the rest of their lives. These reminiscences became a touchstone for them, an easily accessible happiness they can call up at any time.

The planning and experiencing of big gestures take more than five minutes a day. However, the moments of anticipation and memory that come before or after the events are as important as the gifts, trips, or parties and can add to daily enjoyment. Like a stone thrown in a pond, the ripples caused by a big gesture circle out in all directions. Cherishing these moments with each other or just with yourself infuses a feel-good atmosphere into your relationship.

- Take a few minutes to savor the anticipation of an upcoming trip or event. What aspects of it are you most excited about? The relief from your daily grind? A chance to bond with your spouse? Write down these thoughts—it will be enlightening to review them after the big day(s).
- Include your partner in a five-minute discussion about the upcoming experience. Share your eagerness by trading thoughts on how it will be and counting down the days. This sharing enhances a team feeling.
- After the event is over, cherish the memories. Write down specific details about what happened, and who said what, in order to preserve them. Organize and frame the photographs so they don't vanish into a box (or digital file), never to be seen again. Do small amounts every day. It prolongs the good taste.
- When surprising your spouse with a big gift or party, as noted in Chapter 2 it can be tempting to give something that we would want. Will your shy partner really enjoy unsuspectingly walking into a crowded room of

friends and relatives? Will your frugal man feel comfortable receiving a brand new coat? Spend a few minutes putting yourself in the other's shoes and imagining the reaction at the moment of revelation.

- As the years go by, employ the memory of your great day, gift, or event to ease a journey through darker times. Having a rough patch? Wear that gift as a happiness refresher.

- Brainstorm about future big moments you can share. What's coming down the path? A child about to graduate? A big anniversary? Before getting into the details of planning, have brief daily conversations about what would mean the most to you both. Perhaps there aren't enough resources for an anniversary party *and* this year's ski trip. Which would evoke the most fondness upon recall?

- Don't wait. A common truism: No one lies on his death bed wishing he had spent more time at work. Even if money and time are tight, take a few minutes to contemplate how you can invest in a big gesture. Set aside a certain amount of cash a month, or ask your boss if you can take unpaid vacation time to fulfill your family's needs. Of course, the priceless memories of the trip or lifecycle event will outweigh the money and time spent.

Chapter 9

Kid Stuff

Studies show a correlation between having children and a dive in marital satisfaction. It makes sense—remember the joys of long meals, relaxed sex, going to the movies, or sleeping in? Kids mean these enjoyments are a thing of the past, for the moment. Add to these inconveniences financial pressures, clashes over discipline or whose turn it is to get up with the baby, and concerns over letting your sixteen-year-old take the car, and reproduction could seem an unwise endeavor for a contented couple. Yet, many of us are happy, and sometimes desperate, to take this leap of love and faith. Why?

Having children is a worthwhile investment. It may seem hard to believe when the baby is teething or your adolescent swears he hates you, but offspring give meaning to life. Despite the difficulties of the early years, the luckiest of us will forever savor those moments of pride and joy—a baby's first giggle, a teenager being kind to a stranger. Moreover, our later years are blessed with graduations, weddings, and grandkids: the stuff of a full, contented life.

So, how then do you get from here to there? How do you protect your marriage while caring for your children, those perennial squeaky wheels? It's a matter of paying attention with thoughtful purpose. Even five minutes a day can make a real difference in the environment between you and your partner despite the Cheerios crunching under your feet.

Harder Than It Has to Be

Today there is intense pressure to be the ideal parent. Having so much information at our fingertips is obviously advantageous, yet too often we become slaves to the thought of raising a perfect child. Whereas in earlier years, parents relied on family advice, common sense, and intuition, we now spend hours on the Internet in search of the best baby food or diaper solution—and oftentimes we still come away unsatisfied. In addition, comparing your parenting skills to the blogger you admire or the super-competent mom at the park can fill your over-tired mind with dark thoughts of unworthiness and doubt. Enter your laidback mate who forgot Scout's hat once again and doesn't believe the hype about organic this or that and your passion for perfect parenting can quickly turn into an equally passionate rant. Although everyone involved in this scenario has the best of intentions—a healthy, happy kid—a clash of parenting styles can lead to some ugly arguments.

Avoiding such fights can take as little as five minutes a day of prioritization and communication. What is really important to you? Why? Pick one issue that you and your spouse disagree on, something that makes your blood boil every time. Then, before it comes up again, sit down and calmly hash it out. Consider the following dialogue:

"It is important to me that Scout wear his hat whenever he's out in the sun because his baby skin is super-sensitive."

"Between the diaper bag and all his stuff, I sometimes forget his hat. It's not a big deal."

"It's a big deal to me. My grandmother had melanoma and I don't want to take that risk with him. What if I buy a bunch of hats and put one in his bag, one in both cars, and a couple around the house? Will that help?"

"Sure. I didn't know you felt so strongly about it. Since we're on the topic, can you do me a favor?"

"Of course. What?"

"It drives me crazy when you don't wash his bottles as thoroughly as you could. I keep having to go back and redo them. Can you be more careful?"

"I had no idea you were doing that. I'll pay more attention."

Extra Credit

Let's make a deal! Offer to read the book that most agrees with your partner's parenting philosophy. Then, ask her to read yours. Often we can better connect on points of disagreement when the source is someone other than a close loved one.

Being a new parent—or even a veteran mom or dad—can be so overwhelming that you and your spouse may forget to check in with each other to see what behavioral shifts you can make to ensure a happy home. A quick, five-minute dialogue such as the one above could help circumvent an argument that may begin about a hat but can quickly devolve into character attacks due to sleep deprivation and stress. Ease up on yourself and your partner. Yes, you want the best for your kid, but at the end of the day the most important parenting skill is love.

Protecting Your Marriage

Raising children is a full time job. And that means all parents, whether you work outside the home, maintain the home, volunteer, or create art, have more than one job—and that's in addition to caring for your marriage. Why do expressions of love so often take a back seat to daily duties? After all, there are few things more important to a child than having parents who love and support one another.

Think back to the last time you flew on a commercial plane; the stewardess surely emphasized that you should put your oxygen mask on before assisting your child. You can apply this idea to your marriage as well. When you feel guilty about leaving your kids with a babysitter so you can reconnect with your spouse over dinner, remember the lesson of the oxygen mask. You can best protect your children's lives if you are taking care of yourself, and that means enjoying a nurturing relationship with your spouse.

ABE & ROSE'S STORY

Abe and Rose married with stars in their eyes. He began his career as an architect, and she was a midwife. They loved their careers and they loved their life together in the heart of a funky Portland neighborhood. Whenever the mood struck, they went to hear the latest jazz, made love at odd hours, and basically felt like they were in heaven.

But Rose's biological clock was ticking, and within five years they had two beautiful girls and all that went along with them: unlimited cloth diapers, fresh baby food that they made on a daily basis, attempts at keeping their small apartment in order, and almost no sleep. And, after five years with babies in their bed you can imagine what happened to their sex life.

The babies are happy, but Abe and Rose are worn out, overworked, and exhausted. Here's a day in the life: Abe wanted to take a yoga class because his back was going out, and Rose was out of her mind with work in and out of the house.

"Rose, there is a class at 11:00. Do you mind if I go?"

No answer.

Louder: "Rose, can you please say 'yes' or 'no'?"

"Yes or no."

"Thanks a lot—you make me feel guilty. You know my back is killing me."

"Why are you always saying you feel guilty? Are you trying to make *me* feel guilty?"

"I never thought of it that way, but maybe."

"Well, it isn't working."

"I want so much to be healthy for you, to make love to you, to go hear music with you, to eventually find a babysitter so we can be a couple again. Maybe next Saturday we can hear the Sensations at the Blue Note."

"What will happen to the 11 P.M. feeding?"

"Can't you pump?"

"I'll try."

"Thank you. See you later."

This brief discussion demonstrates the goodwill that Abe and Rose have for each other, despite their exhaustion. So, have these children ruined a wonderful relationship? Yes and no. Abe and Rose will bounce back if they continue a give-and-take like the conversation above demonstrates. And hopefully in the future they will have many proud moments, lots of satisfying milestones with children and grandchildren, as well as the bond of having been in the trenches together. It is more than possible that eventually Rose and Abe will have time to rekindle what they once had.

Know the Difference Between Joy and Happiness

Bringing children into the world and nurturing them responsibly is your contribution to improving the world and making it a better place for all of us. Raising children is part of your bequest and your grasp at immortality. For those who cannot or choose not to have offspring, your legacy and life meaning can be found in a myriad of other pathways. But for the majority of us, it is our obligation to provide the world with responsible, creative citizens. So take five minutes a day to commit to your idealism, do your bit to save the world, and just appreciate the joy of being alive. Taking for granted anything in life whether it is the fresh bread you are eating, the giggles of the grandchildren, or seeing the sunset, is a foolish and blind way of living.

Choosing to have children is a complicated, personal decision that cuts to the heart of the difference between happiness and joy. Happiness is transient. It is the fun meal out, the day at the spa. Joy is deeper—and more challenging. With joy often comes struggle, but when you get to the other side, it provides deep satisfaction.

Five-Minute Strategies

Children offer moments of bliss, despite the difficulties they sometimes bring to a marriage. With generosity and good communication, even for just a few minutes a day, you can keep your marriage on track while pursuing the joys of family life. These five minutes are an investment in staying together, for the sake of the kids, yes, but also for each other. By making a daily effort to check in with one another, despite your stress or exhaustion, you will go far in creating a home environment that is peaceful and loving.

- Offer your partner the gift of time. Having children can be so overwhelming that you might forget to take your own needs into account. And, if you're always tired or continually deprived of a good chat with a friend, you'll have few resources for good spousal communication. Urge your spouse to go take a nap, get her nails done, or see a movie with a friend.
- Plan a date night. This advice is repeated because it works. Call the babysitter and the restaurant and look forward to Saturday night. No guilt allowed! Sure, you'll probably spend most of the evening discussing the kids, but you won't be interrupted by anyone else's needs. Take this opportunity to honestly discuss your experience of becoming a parent. It may help you connect if you both let down your guard and admit you are overwhelmed or scared.
- Voice your gratitude for your partner's hard work by saying something like, "I know how tough it is to coach the little league during your day off. I really appreciate

how tirelessly you are working." Acknowledgment can go far toward each of you feeling appreciated and can take the sting out of another sleepless night.

- Curtail ugly arguments by taking a break. Sleep deprivation and stress can turn a simple discussion into a character assassination. When you feel yourself (or notice your partner) becoming irrational, offer to take a five-minute break from the discussion and reapproach it when you are both calmer and better rested.

- Rough night? A big, sympathetic hug shows you are a team. Don't try to compare your all-nighter from a week ago in an attempt to one-up her. Let your spouse vent and lay her weary head on your shoulder. Let her know that you agree this is hard, but it will get better.

- Have a sense of humor. Even the toughest moments can be alleviated by a good laugh. Is she crying out of exhaustion, breasts leaking all over her shirt? Get your own shirt just as soaked to show your damp camaraderie. A smile is guaranteed.

Chapter 10

Money Matters

Even in the best of times, money is a common source of conflict for married couples. But when necessary you must do what you can to turn lemons into lemonade. If circumstances have led to more time at home with less purchasing power, how can you exploit this to realize that the best things in life are free? You can do this by resisting the stress of the outside world and stubbornly buckling down to create happiness in your marriage, despite a strained financial situation. Spending just five minutes a day on instituting behavioral changes can have a lasting impact on the development of an atmosphere of love and mutual respect where peace of mind is more highly revered than money. This is not easy, especially in marriages where there are children, but it is essential.

Tensions on the Rise

Possessing less money, less job security, or no job at all is admittedly tough on any marriage. Divvying up a smaller and smaller piece of the pie becomes an enormous source of personal stress when bills still need to be paid and groceries bought—not to mention the high cost of raising children. Scrimping to make ends meet is not even remotely romantic or fun.

Emotionally, couples might hit a roadblock if one partner is working to support the family and the other is out of a job. The latter may feel depressed or defensive. "I sent out twenty resumes today. What do you want from me?" The spouse heading off to work each day could resent his partner's ability to sleep late. It becomes too easy to wonder: "What exactly is she doing all day while I'm being yelled at by my boss? Only twenty resumes? She should have sent out fifty!"

The key to overcoming this type of tension is remembering to give your partner the benefit of the doubt, which prioritizes the family environment over the economic world environment. By taking five minutes a day to put yourself in your spouse's shoes, it will become apparent that both of you are doing your best in a difficult situation. As you head home at the end of the day, take a few minutes on your commute or in your driveway to consider your spouse's best qualities. Breathe deeply and enter your home in a peaceful frame of mind, blame-free. If you are the partner looking for work, you can also take five minutes at the end of the day to pat yourself on the back for having the courage to be vulnerable. Approach your partner's return with a sense of gratitude.

A Spender vs. a Saver

Another common source of financial tension arises when one spouse is comfortable spending money, while the other would rather save. Our feelings about money are often rooted in our original families. If your dad was frequently out of work and you grew up watching mom urgently hunt through the coupon section, you may still have a lingering sense that there will never be enough money to feel secure. You save and save for a rainy day that may never come, missing out on stimulating experiences.

On the flip side, those who are spenders to the point of carelessness often grew up without effective financial guidance. Lessons about saving and credit card overuse were missed. As adults, financial trouble looms as cars pile up in the garage and the house is excessively mortgaged. We all fall somewhere along the spend/save continuum. If you have a tendency to spend and your spouse saves, you may find yourself clashing over financial decisions. Use the table below to see where you fall on the spend/save continuum:

Spender	Happy Medium	Saver
My five-year-old laptop works fine, but is basically obsolete. Time to get the latest model.	For a computer, it is old. I'm going to take it to my computer guy to clean it up, reinstall the operating system and upgrade my software. That should buy me a few more years.	If it ain't broke, why worry about it? I plan on using this computer until it dies.
My friends are renting a villa in Tuscany for two weeks. I don't have the money, but this is a once-in-a-lifetime opportunity. I'll just charge it.	I may be able to swing going to Italy for five days, rather than two weeks. I'll work a couple extra shifts so I can have some spending money.	Plane fare aside, the dollar is worth half what a Euro is worth. I'd rather go down to the shore for two weeks than risk overspending.
It's our tenth anniversary, and I want to get her something special. I know she'll say we can't afford it, but I'm going to splurge on that antique armoire she admired.	I know she's expecting something special, but this is not the time for a big expensive gesture. I'll get her those silver earrings and splurge on a nice dinner.	Our love doesn't require spending a lot of money. She should be thrilled at my handwritten card and the lasagna I made from scratch.

A spender and a saver can actually balance one another out, if each of you is flexible enough to accept that the other has a valid point of view. Spenders can help the more frugal partner learn happiness in the present. Take five minutes to make your case for loosening the purse strings by clipping out images of your dream vacation from magazines, or telling the story of the fun your colleague and her husband have on their bikes. Savers, ask when your partner has a few minutes for an IRA discussion. When he agrees to a sit down, explain how yearly contributions will grow into a nice sum for future security or retirement.

Extra Credit
Consider enlisting a financial advisor who can help you create a sound investment strategy. Having a third party expert in the picture can lessen the likelihood of clashing over money.

Financial solvency is of course preferable to a zero balance, yet for many people the amount in the bank they consider "enough" keeps being raised and it soon becomes meaningless. As they say, you can't take it with you. Consider the following quote from University of Illinois Professor Emeritus of Psychology Ed Diener: "Yes, money makes you happy—we see the effect of income on life satisfaction is very strong and virtually ubiquitous and universal around the world. But it makes you more satisfied than it makes you feel good. Positive feelings are less affected by money and more affected by the things people are doing day-to-day."

STUART & VANESSA'S STORY

In Vanessa and Stuart's marriage, all control of bill paying, expenditures, savings, and investing was in the hands of Vanessa, an accountant in a large firm. She had faith in her investment advisor, Kyle, and for a time Vanessa and Kyle were working well together.

Recently the market took a downturn and Stuart lost his job as a screenwriter. With three children in their teens, he was happy to be Mr. Mom as he missed out on the early years. But then tensions began between Vanessa and Stuart over their nest egg. Once he was home, he was happy to take over the daily details including running the expenses and investment portfolio. Stuart said their advisor, Kyle, did a sloppy job and they lost half their hard-earned savings. Vanessa believed that he did the best he could in a volatile market. She was annoyed with Stuart as he surrendered fiscal autonomy to her and then blamed her for trusting Kyle.

Stuart's resentment toward Vanessa was waylaid when he began reading studies about consumption and happiness, which overwhelmingly show that people are happier when they spend money on experiences instead of objects. Influenced by the research, Stuart decided to forget about the income and savings defeat and devise experiences that he, Vanessa, and the children could share.

"Listen, Vanessa, the past is the past. In fact, I think our losses have been a wakeup call for our family."

"Oh, really? Why do you say that?"

"I've been doing some reading, and the old cliché that money doesn't buy happiness seems to be true. It's time and shared experiences that make life worthwhile. Let's take the kids to Yosemite this weekend. What do you think?"

"I love it! And, I love you."

What Really Makes Us Happy

Whatever you shell out big bucks for, whether it be a new home, car, or the latest fashions, the thrill lasts a week, a day, or a minute. We quickly acclimate to our new purchases, which is why it's easy to become dissatisfied. Before long, we need the bigger house and the better car. Consumers and marketers exist in a never-ending loop. Instead of providing happiness, our desire for consumption has endowed credit card companies with huge profits. How can we stop the madness?

A 2009 study published in *Family Relations* shows that "core family leisure activities," such as going on a picnic with the kids, playing board games, or just heading out for a long drive, increases feelings of togetherness. These low-cost activities are recession-proof! This same study reflects the benefits of experiences that occur less often, but cost money. These "Balance Family Activities," such as travel or cultural events, encourage newness and adaptability. The substantial outlay on a ski vacation or cruise with your loved one is an investment in memory-making. Spend five minutes today exploring the next adventure you want to share with your spouse.

Interestingly, despite rising financial tensions among married couples, the divorce rate is declining. But before we smile at this good news, let's consider why: It's too expensive. So, couples are less happy during financial strife, but these same dire straits bind them together. An April 2010 report from the Council on Contemporary Families states, "We know from the experience of the Great Depression of the 1930s that divorce rates can fall while family conflict and domestic violence rates rise." This phenomenon affords many couples the opportunity to discover how to enjoy what they have rather than cutting ties. And, hopefully, with the help of the lessons imparted in this book, they will come out the other side more in love than ever.

Five-Minute Strategies

As unromantic as it sounds, marriage is a financial contract. Unfortunately, many people exchange vows without ever discussing their financial habits, debts, and economic goals, which only lay the groundwork for conflict down the road. Luckily, there are several daily strategies for learning how to better approach the nexus of your financial life and your marriage. Most important is taking five minutes to overcome knee-jerk impulses when it comes to money—whether that means holding on to it too tightly or spending too freely.

- Initiate a brief conversation with your partner about how your parents handled money as you were growing up. Knowing this piece of history will be illuminating and may explain why your wife saves every paperclip or why your husband can't stop buying nonsense on eBay. Once you have an understanding of your partner's past, it will be easier to access empathy.
- Most of us live in dual-income households, but one person will always bring in more income than the other. If you're the main earner, take five minutes to give your partner the benefit of the doubt about how hard he is working. This may mean taking time before encountering each other to recall his best qualities.
- Don't let resentment build. If one of you is the primary breadwinner, and the other works fewer hours or pursues a passion that isn't a big money-maker, suggest other, nonfiduciary ways he can contribute. Perhaps one of you does more childcare or handles all the shopping.

- Share your ideas of what you can *experience* together instead of spending your money on a new gadget or pair of shoes. Take five minutes to each write down three activities that cost less than $50 that you would enjoy. Then, look at the calendar and plan on doing them. Game night, mini golf, hiking, and people-watching downtown are just some of the fun pursuits at your fingertips.

- Entice your spendthrift spouse with ideas for spending money that can augment her happiness. What does she enjoy, but resists purchasing because she feels it would be too self-indulgent? Cut out pictures from magazines and surreptitiously place them where she will find them. Or, plan a shopping trip and tell her it's her special day and you insist she buy something she will cherish.

- Explain to your shopaholic partner how his overspending makes you feel insecure about the future. Describe your investment strategies so he is on board. There are plenty of good books on investing and saving for retirement that can help you make your case.

- Avoid being secretive about your financial life. Often, one spouse handles the bills and accounts for the household. If you don't see eye-to-eye with your partner on money, it can be tempting to keep a lid on exactly how much money you have, where it is, and how it's spent. This is dangerous in that it can build resentment and, if you die before your partner, he will be in the dark. Have a financial check-in once a month or quarter. If you make a habit of this, it only takes a few minutes to fill your partner in on the family accounts.

Chapter 11

Happy Differences

You were initially attracted to your partner for your differences as well as your similarities. Perhaps you were intrigued by her exotic religious upbringing, while you remain an atheist. Maybe his intellectual roots contrasted happily with your blue-collar family. In addition, many couples are opposites even if on the surface their childhoods seem comparable. As you grow and change together, profound personality differences can come to light: one is shy, while the other is outgoing; one likes adventure while the other enjoys the security of home.

These differences can be a source of happiness if you allow them to keep you intrigued with your partner. Creating a life with someone who is unlike yourself can be stimulating; it can keep you humble, and encourage flexibility. But, if you don't evolve, or if you thwart your partner's evolution, your long-term happiness is at stake.

Fear of Loss

The price to pay for living with someone whose beliefs, values, or behavioral norms contrast with your own is conflict. You may feel annoyed or frustrated by the way your spouse approaches a situation ("Why does she always have to bring up politics with my family?" "Can't he be on time for once?"). But, on a fundamental level, what you may really sense is a fear of loss. When your loved one exercises his right to differ, awareness of the chasm that separates you may be vivid—no matter how much love there is in your relationship. After all, if your partner can differ so greatly from you, can you ever really know him? Who's to say this person won't just up and walk out the door someday?

These fears generally operate under the radar. If your other half is not enthusiastic about Christmas, yet you gleefully wear red and green from Thanksgiving to New Year's, you probably don't knowingly fear abandonment. However, this unbridgeable gap may fill you with frustration and sometimes anger. You decorate the tree alone, fuming as he serenely watches football. Underneath this picture is fear that togetherness is fragile, that you are ultimately on your own in the universe.

How to Make Your Differences Happy

When differences arise, take five minutes to be open-minded about why your partner feels a certain way about money, food, religion, or whatever the issue is. Asking nonjudgmental questions such as "I find it interesting that we feel so differently on this subject. How do you experience the divide?" can open the door to understanding.

The key to building a link on subjects that are highly emotional is dealing with them for five minutes a day—and no more—with minimal off-putting emotion. Put one brick on the foundation of the bridge, study it, and then go play tennis, take a walk, or make love. Change the subject; it registered. No need to hit your partner over the head with your impassioned point of view. That only serves to create a wall between you as he must protect himself from your onslaught.

SAY THIS

"I appreciate how hard it is for us to see eye-to-eye on this. Please know that no matter how we resolve this issue, I love you and will not leave you."

The Five-Minute Barter

Another communication tactic for handling differences is a five-minute barter. Staying together involves much give-and-take, and often a peaceful way to resolve a conflict is to offer your cooperation in exchange for your spouse's. A few small steps toward each other's point of view often result in a happy meeting of the mind.

> *Extra Credit*
>
> Perhaps you absolutely hate modern jazz. Or, your Catholicism precludes you joining him for services at his synagogue. Just try it. Showing interest and trying out something that you wouldn't do otherwise is a show of good faith.

For instance, say staying close to family is important to you, but your partner does not want to spend every Sunday with your parents. His college buddies feel more like family to him, and he wants to go to the West Coast twice a year to visit. You resent the expense and separation. In five minutes, you could work out a system where he agrees to host your parents once a month and you agree that he includes you on one of his jaunts west. This compromise will bridge an understanding of what *family* means to both of you.

MAYA & IBRAHIM'S STORY

Ibrahim was a lawyer determined to make partner at his firm. His wife, Maya, understood why he worked so hard, but often felt lonely due to his travel schedule and late hours. In addition, she didn't feel comfortable at the conservative firm's social functions, where she and Ibrahim were always the sole Muslim couple. One Sunday afternoon, Ibrahim approached Maya with a request, but feared she would be upset.

"Maya, I want to speak to you about something important connected to the firm. When can we have five minutes together?"

"Let's take a walk around the block. It's beautiful out."

Outside, he continued, "The firm has asked me to take on an important assignment which means for the next three months I will have to be in Brazil for ten days on, four days off, and then back again."

Maya paused, and then said, "I will miss you very much, but I understand how important your career is, and I will support you."

"Wow. Thank you."

"And now I have something to discuss which is very difficult for me and very pressing."

"Go ahead."

"Since my parents are coming from Indonesia to stay with us for six months, and since my mother is observant, I would like to cover my head while she is here. I know how much you do not want to disrupt your law firm's image of you as a moderate Muslim—their showpiece for investors and clients—and I appreciate this. On the other hand, I do not want to offend my parents. Take some time to think about it and let's speak again in a few days. Thank you for listening without interrupting. It makes me feel respected and hopeful."

During their five-minute walk around the block, Maya and Ibrahim approached some key differences in their marriage—his need to travel for work, and Maya wanting to be more observant than he wanted. Notice how the conversation was brief and the couple's emotions were kept even-keeled. This gave both of them a chance to digest the other's need while avoiding impassioned debate.

Learning to Bend

The more flexible you are, the more embracing of your partner's differences, the happier you'll be. Encouraging your spouse to evolve is a loving gesture, especially if you find it difficult to muster up enthusiasm for his aspirations. (Of course, this is not to say you can support actions that you deem negative such as drug abuse or other destructive habits.) But many couples who come to my office approach their differences with rigidity rather than flexibility. When they refuse to decipher the value of their partner's method of disciplining their child or money management, a wall is erected, cutting off constructive dialogue.

Being flexible means losing this my-way-or-the-highway approach. In most instances, there is no single right method to handling a situation. Putting yourself in your spouse's shoes is an exercise that can go a long way toward increasing mutual understanding. Even if it makes you uncomfortable, for five minutes a day, notice how your partner faces a situation over which you usually clash. Is she always late because she's trying to look beautiful for you? Does he overspend because he was poor growing up and it brings him joy? Is he quiet at the end of the day because his job is overwhelming? Approach your spouse's differences with empathy rather than aggression—and watch love bloom.

Five-Minute Strategies

People are moving targets. This fact can be both fascinating and frustrating in a long-term marriage. Happiness is more likely if you find the differences between you and your partner (not to mention the differences between the person you married and this *same* person decades later!) to be stimulating rather than exasperating. This will require five-minute exercises in avoiding judgment and accessing empathy. In five minutes, you can choose to admire, accept, or at the very least be resigned to your spouse's differences. Remember: Appreciating the differences between you and your spouse prevents you from merging and giving up your personal boundaries, which can lead to unhappiness. Enjoy the stimulating fact that you are both unique individuals!

- Ask a nonjudgmental question about why your partner feels differently from you. Be careful to watch your tone during this exchange. If this is a longstanding difference, you may have to overcome a bit of resistance in your partner. Encouragement and patience are key.
- Offer your opinion on the subject at hand without being overemotional. After five minutes, change the topic—go for a run or begin dinner; keeping your talks short will lessen the likelihood of a big blow-up. This will give both of you time to consider each other's point of view. Over time, these five-minute conversations will allow you to reach an understanding about where you both are coming from.
- Timing is everything so choose the moment to have your discussion carefully. Discussing differences, especially

hot-button disparities on such issues as politics, religion, or child rearing, requires a velvet touch. Take a few minutes to gauge whether or not your partner is in a mood that fosters openness. If so, broach the subject. If he's overwhelmed, exhausted, or distracted, save your talk for a more opportune moment.

- Engage in a five-minute give-and-take. Marriage often involves cooperation. Once you understand your partner's viewpoint you may have to give something up to get what you desire. And isn't what you ultimately want a harmonious feeling of closeness?

- Be flexible rather than rigid. For five minutes a day, put yourself in your partner's shoes, giving him the benefit of the doubt. Notice when you feel yourself becoming resistant, digging your heels in over a certain issue. Devise a strategy that helps you to access your flexibility such as deep breathing or laughter. Once you feel more open and relaxed, approach your partner with empathy at the ready.

- Ironically, the things you loved about your partner back in the day may have become the exact diversity over which you now clash. When you are tempted to create a conflict over what you once loved but now perceive as a difference, take five minutes to remember a time when you accepted this aspect of your partner. Use that happy memory to access your acceptance today.

PART 3

Five-Minute Strategies for Great Communication

Chapter 12

Body Language

Along the bumpy road of love, much of the way you communicate with your partner is nonverbal. The disapproving look your wife gives you when you order dessert, the way your husband clenches his fists in frustration: All these gestures send signals that couldn't be clearer. And because our emotions are so in synch with our bodies, nonverbal expressions often tell all. People are usually unaware of the impact this silent language has on others. But consider, does standing with your arms folded over your chest invite open communication? How will your sex life stay on track if you flinch at her touch?

It is crucial to remain conscious of what you are nonverbally communicating. Without this awareness, you and your partner risk alienating each other with thoughtless gestures. Take a few minutes a day to pay close attention to your body language. You may be surprised to discover how it affects and reflects the harmony in your marriage.

Reading Your Partner

Understanding your partner's body language is a window into, if not his soul, then at least his everyday moods and desires. Take a few minutes before engaging to step back and read what is being said. Does his posture suggest he needs some space? Are those tears in her eyes saying a hug would be appreciated? If you're not sure what to look out for, here are some clues to help you decode your partner's body language.

Action	Meaning
Arms crossed at chest level	"I am closed off."
Hands on hips	"I am open to conversation." Or, "I dare you."
Shoulders back, hands at side	"I am relaxed and welcome a good talk."
Eyes wide open	"I'm surprised" Or, "I'm scared."
Shrug	"This is not so important." Or, "You caught me." (defensive)

We instantly recognize the emotions in other people's facial expressions. Psychologist Paul Ekman, in his book *The Nature of Emotion*, expands on Charles Darwin's observations that the expressions of basic emotions are universal. Ekman conducted research that supports Darwin's conclusions by showing a set of photographs of faces expressing happiness, disgust, surprise, fear, sadness, and anger to people in cultures across the world. A smiling face most societies regarded as happy. This universal recognition was also true for sadness and disgust.

As in a game of poker, everyone has their tell, and it can be fun to discover your partner's specific quirks. (Perhaps she sucks her teeth or twists her rings when she's nervous.) Knowing the meaning behind the gesture increases intimacy; it becomes a private language. In addition, you can avoid unpleasant encounters by noting that your spouse is wordlessly expressing tension or stress. (Now may not be the ideal time to bring up the new dent in the car!) Challenge yourself to step back for five minutes a day and watch and learn. The more you become aware of the unspoken current that flows between you, the better you will be able to understand and manage your interpersonal connections.

What Are You Really Saying?

Learning your spouse's body language is only half the battle. *Your* body is also a participant in the dance. It folds and unfolds, clenches and relaxes, reaches out and holds back. With daily practice, you can become attentive to how you are silently expressing yourself, and modify your gestures if they do not reflect what you were hoping to communicate or trigger an unintended response from your spouse.

If you think of your relationship as a dance, consider how your body responds to your spouse's. Who leads? Emotions tend to be contagious, so when your husband comes home full of stress and worry, do you reflect those feelings? Do you experience your shoulders tensing up at the sight of his furrowed brow? Mirror neurons in our brains imitate the other person's mood. When you become aware of this inadvertent response, you can consciously choose another option to help ease negative feelings without saying anything at all. Use your physicality to change the mood. It takes less than five minutes to give him an open smile and a warm hug, hold your arms loosely at your side, and watch his body release its tense stance as your mirror neurons influence the environment.

After a lifetime, your physical being habitually reflects your emotions. Staying conscious of how you move is empowering. An interesting exercise is to take a video camera and record a five-minute conversation between you and your spouse, or look at spontaneous snapshots of your life together. You may be shocked at what you see. Do your gestures invite loving communication, or do you move away, look at him with contempt, or not meet his gaze at all? This undeniable proof of how you move together can be a surprising and possibly humbling inspiration for a fresh start.

LEON & BETSY'S STORY

Betsy complained that Leon's gestures were violent and frightening. She cited many nonverbal forms of hostility such as throwing wine from his glass, and closing and opening a front door near her ankle. She feels that he mainly threatened her with his body language. From Leon 's point of view, he would rather hurt himself than physically abuse a woman. He became so irritated when feeling unappreciated by Betsy that his actions and body language were simply expressions of futility. Betsy grew up in a household where corporal punishment was the medium for disciplining the children. Leon's behavior is an unpleasant reminder of her strict upbringing.

Betsy and Leon arrived at my office tense but ready to talk. She began, "I don't want to live in a house where I feel threatened all the time. Your behavior is extreme."

Taking a deep breath, Leon said, "It's not as if I plan to slam the door or break the dish, I just get so frustrated I don't know what else to do."

"Well, it scares me."

"Okay, I get it. But you can help by supporting me while I'm out of work instead of nagging me all the time. I'm discouraged enough and need to feel loved at home."

"I'm sorry. I didn't realize that. I'll try to do my best to be more supportive."

"So will I."

"Sounds like a plan."

Leon and Betsy have taken a first step toward addressing the problem of how their negative physicality was hurting their marriage. Their marriage was a closed circuit where positive energy elicits positive energy. For example, if Betsy is warmer; Leon states he would feel more supported and be less likely to lash out. Yet in reality each partner must be responsible for his own reactivity. It is not up to Betsy to curb Leon's bad temper; it is up to him. And Betsy's need for safety first had to come from her confidence in herself, should all else fail.

It's All in the Eyes

One of the biggest lessons I impart to my clients is to look at one another with the intent of accessing warmth. Once you stare into your partner's eyes your anger often melts, replaced with giggles or empathic connection. Just looking with positive intention has a deepening effect on relationships. When you are willing to gaze at your partner, you increase the chances of being able to read him without speaking. Take five minutes today and sit down for a brief conversation with your spouse, eye contact mandatory. Notice how the connection between you is heightened, how even if you are discussing something mundane, smiles tend to ensue.

Extra Credit

Too often, people choose long car rides to have an important discussion, and it's difficult to maintain consistent eye contact when one of you is driving. Instead, engage in important discussions in a place where you can face each other and look in each other's eyes, such as a café or your couch.

It's always a happy moment when you and your partner lock eyes across a room and feel like you are on the same wavelength. The comfort that comes from not having to spell everything out harkens back to our early years before we had language. Of course, our children are taught to "use their words" instead of enacting them. But nevertheless there is no greater pleasure than tapping into the baby that exists in all of us. For most people, when a loved one acknowledges something needed or wanted without having to "use our words," the bliss reminiscent of preverbal contentment ensues.

However, not all eye contact is positive. There is a difference between looking at someone judgmentally and with good judgment. Nothing need be said when your spouse orders one drink too many and you give him *the* look. He experiences your disapproval, and may feel reactively rebellious enough to order more. Most people rail against being controlled. Similarly, you catch his eye roll when your friend who he considers ditsy arrives. *But she has a good heart*, you think to yourself, resenting his nonverbal critique. Appearing judgmental is silently destructive in a marriage.

Looking at someone with good judgment, on the other hand, is a nonverbal gesture that strengthens love. By respecting your spouse's autonomy, you wisely understand that you can't change anyone's behavior besides your own. So, when she orders the fries instead of the salad, resist giving her a meaningful look that says, "I don't know why we bother to pay for the gym if you're going to eat like this." Instead, look with compassion, humor, and trust. Perhaps she's planning on working out twice as long to make up for the French fries. In any case, the decision isn't up to you, so why inject the moment with negativity?

If you're on the other end of a judgmental look, try to just visualize standing on your own and become centered in who you are. This gives you the ability to convert a disapproving glance into a funny quirk. If you can do this, you won't care if you get the look when you order your French fries.

The power of body language in a marriage cannot be underestimated. Practice daily to increase awareness of how you and your partner silently communicate. A few minutes a day of conscious attention, chosen at a consistent time in which to notice how you dance can have lasting power. At breakfast, do you make eye contact, touch hands, or do you maintain your gaze on the paper, keeping your arms to yourself? If your love isn't being expressed by your physicality, it's up to you to change course!

Body language happens in an instant, but has a cumulative effect on a marriage. Whereas you once may have consistently expressed your love through touch and an open, nonjudgmental gaze, this positive physicality may have slowly faded with time. For this reason, the key five-minute strategy here is maintaining awareness, both of your own and your partner's body language. Once you've trained yourself to pay attention, you can tweak your expressiveness in order to enhance the feeling of devotion in your marriage.

- Take a few minutes to notice your spouse's nonverbal lingo before engaging in a conversation. This awareness can go far in supporting a positive interaction. If you perceive her as tense or angry, it may be wise to back off and choose a more opportune time for interaction.
- Take a few minutes a day and focus on your body language and what it's saying. Pick a time—over lunch or in a meeting—and focus on how you move. Are you hunched over with your arms folded, or are you more open with your shoulders back, inviting interaction? Does your body language match the emotion you want to express? If you want to have more control of the vibe you are sending other people, daily awareness is crucial. Practice in front of the mirror so your muscle memory can play a part in rewiring how you physically express emotion.
- Moods are contagious, so be aware of the power of your nonverbal communication. If you walk into the house with your gaze averted and your arms crossed, you can

expect a happy vibe to fade as your spouse catches your emotional signals. The other option? If you've had a bad day, take a few minutes before you walk in the door to relax your body: Do some facial exercises, touch your toes. Then, walk in with a smile, happy to be home.

- Videotape a five-minute conversation between you and your spouse and witness how you relate through gestures. Or, go through old snapshots with the goal of viewing your nonverbal expressions. You may be surprised at your discoveries! If you see yourself unwittingly expressing a negative emotion or signal, practice rewiring your body language on a daily basis.

- Talk to your spouse with consistent eye contact. Even if it's uncomfortable at first, commit to a mutual gaze and see how long it takes you to break into a smile. Make an effort to have important conversations in an environment where you can meet each other's eyes; this will heighten your communication.

- Don't give in to judgmental looks, even if you feel your partner's behavior is maddening. When tempted, take a few minutes to acknowledge your desire to judge or control and transform this with the choice to gaze compassionately. Remember: You can't change other people, only yourself.

- Think of your body language as a dance with your partner. How each of you moves has a direct effect on the other's physicality. These movements are powerful expressions of your emotions. Each day, take a few minutes to observe your dance and make changes if you feel your bodies do not support the health of your relationship.

Chapter 13

Stay Curious

Imagine two young lovers at a café. Chatting happily, they spy an older couple across the room silently sipping their coffees. "That will never be us," is their passionate promise to stay engaged, to remain mutually entertaining. (Of course the young lovers are assuming that silence between people who know each other well is not comfortable engagement.) Now flash forward ten years. Has our couple kept their pledge? Is there anything new to say? Will she endure his one-sided conversation about Fantasy Football? Can he stifle a yawn as she again recounts her wild days in the city?

When you choose to spend your life with someone you risk hearing the same old jokes, the same stories of childhood, the same exaggerated tales of successes and failures. You risk boredom. The good news is that it is actually within *your* power to overcome the tedium of your partner's supposedly unchanging ways. Showing curiosity for how the same stories and jokes come up again and again can shine a light on where your partner is and who he is becoming. Taking an interest in a subject that fascinates your spouse, but that makes you long to close your eyes, is an expression of open-minded curiosity as well as maturity. Of course, you don't have to be enthralled with each other's every hobby. Different people enjoy different things.

But daily, five-minute offerings of inclusive inquisitiveness prevent a life lived on parallel tracks.

Don't Assume You Know

People are constantly changing, which means that you can choose to counteract boredom in your relationship by remaining interested in who your partner is now. Suppose your husband is really interested in politics and reads the newspaper religiously. Spend time getting his take on what he believes will happen next to the government and perhaps how it will affect the world at large. Or suppose your wife just got home from a fashion show of a new young designer. Ask her about what she loved in the show and why. Or after seeing a film together, go to a coffee shop and ask each other what you made of the characters. Too often our partners' behavior, motivations, and intentions become static in our minds. Rather than accepting that you have no idea why your wife is late (traffic? long meeting? inconsideration?), you assume you know. "She's so selfish, always making me wait," you think. A better—and more peaceful—strategy is to give her the benefit of the doubt, remaining interested rather than accusatory. This is an example of personal flexibility that can help you stay unlocked to the potential within your partner. Rigidity, on the other hand, fuels monotony. ("She *always* does x." "I *know* he really means y.") This so-called predictability of interpretation ensures your partner will eventually become less interesting.

Researcher Todd Kashdan's book *Curious?* addresses curiosity in intimate relationships. He writes: "An increase in social approach behaviors, such as being responsive and asking questions, can lead to more novel information about one's partner, and thus to greater feelings of pleasure and attraction." Staying curious on a daily basis means overcoming a tendency to assume. The next time your spouse engages in a typical behavior, take five minutes to explore your belief about what is really going on. Stay open, inquisitive, and inquiring (using a nonjudgmental tone) about the reasons behind the action. You may be surprised at what you discover.

SAY THIS

"I notice this is something you do often. We've lived together a long time and I've never asked you why. Thanks for indulging my curiosity."

FRANK & BARBARA'S STORY

For twenty-eight years, Frank was exasperated by his wife Barbara's propensity to chat up strangers. Frank did not understand the point of engaging with people they were unlikely to ever see again, and the fact that the time it took often made them late frustrated him. He usually stood by while they discussed the weather, the baby, what ever. Last month, Frank and Barbara went out for ice cream. As Frank walked toward the door, cone in hand, he looked back to see Barbara happily chatting with an older woman at a table. Exasperated, he went out to the street to wait. Five minutes passed; ten minutes passed. Frank fumed.

As Barbara emerged, Frank immediately snarled, "Nice that you would rather talk to that strange woman rather than enjoying your ice cream with me."

"Is that what you think?"

"Yes. You are always wasting time with perfect strangers."

"Well, that woman babysat for me until I was ten years old. I haven't seen her for years, and it was meaningful for me to catch up. She went away without saying good-bye to us, and that really hurt. You don't always know, Frank."

Chagrined, Frank apologized, "I guess I just assumed."

The less curiosity that Frank showed toward his wife's way of thinking and the more he assumed that he always knew what was going on, the more their marriage lost its glow.

When Interests Collide

You may have noticed that couples are often interested in activities that they would never choose if they were not with their partners. After all, not everyone shares an equal passion for literature, art, or violent movies. For five minutes a day, fight your initial impulse to roll your eyes at your husband's analysis of the book he is reading or his theory on how the artwork of living artists is more exciting to collect than that of dead ones. Show curiosity as to how violent films or complex economic theories, for example, are interesting.

Imagine your partner is an attractive person who happens to be sitting next to you on a long plane ride. (Which, metaphorically, he is.) Most of the journey you will be listening to music, sleeping, watching a movie, or reading. But for five minutes choose to give your seatmate your attention. He is reading an economics journal. You say, "I don't want to disturb you, but I noticed you are reading something that it would never occur to me to pick up. What do you find interesting about this journal?" Then spend five minutes listening. Thank him for taking his attention away from his reading and then go back to whatever is of interest to you.

SAY THIS

"This enthusiasm of yours is part of who you are. I am open to what interests you because I love you."

In this reverie, you have offered the warmth of human connection, which provides a good feeling on a long ride, and you have also given yourself a window into a new world. Active listening is the key to engaging your spouse in a manner that reflects your unrestricted love. For example, even if you hate violent films, you can approach her fervor for them as an interesting personality quirk. What is it that attracts her to this genre? What does it reveal? What does your dislike of these films indicate about you?

Look at the Part You're Playing

Help your spouse remain curious about *your* interests and passions by treading lightly. Do you notice your husband's eyes wander when you really get going on a certain subject? Is your wife stifling a yawn as you go on and on? Your partner may be a captive audience, but that doesn't mean she is captivated by your every word. Pay attention to body language and, if you feel your audience is losing interest, you do have a couple of options. The first approach is to ask your spouse directly why she is disinterested. For example you could say, "I couldn't help but notice your eyes are wandering. Why aren't we connecting on this topic?"

However, it might be time to just change the subject. Take a step back and revisit your preferred topic at a later time. Ask an open-ended question in order to re-engage your partner in a new direction: "What's going on at work?" "How was your bridge game?" "What's happening with you today?" But don't be surprised if you are met with resistance. Many people experience these questions as intruding. But no matter whether your partner easily opens up or fights your connection to her, do not give up trying.

Remaining curious about the person you love can be oddly challenging because most people assume, after all this time, that they know them inside and out. But, we are continually changing and potentially full of surprises. It only takes a few minutes a day to remain open to how amazing your partner really is. Heraclitus (the ancient Greek philosopher) famously said, "You can't step in the same stream twice." This applies to every long-term marriage. It's wonderfully challenging that we get to reacquaint ourselves with each other as time moves on.

Five-Minute Strategies

In a split second, we often assume we know what our partners are thinking, where they are going with the conversation, or why they behave the way they do. This places our loved ones in a box where they are static, held in place by what we imagine to be true. You may be right to suppose that she's in a bad mood because of PMS, but perhaps not. What if it's job trouble, a rude driver, or she's missing her sister? If you don't inquire, you'll never know. If you can pause and take five minutes to challenge your presuppositions and remain curious about whom your partner is becoming, he will remain vibrant and interesting. This involves daily active listening and patience.

- Combat rigidity by catching yourself when your mind uses words like, *always*, *never*, and *typical*. Assuming your partner is "always" sloppily dressed, "never" on time, and "typically" selfish avoids the complex realities of human behavior. Take five minutes to challenge your assumptions by being flexible and offering your spouse the benefit of the doubt.

- Avoid assuming you know the reasons behind your spouse's behavior. Go ahead and ask. If you broach the subject with openhearted curiosity, your partner may appreciate the chance to voice his motivations. Most people enjoy being given the opportunity to explore why they do what they do. He may even be unaware of his behavior or the reasons behind it and, due to your curious prodding, he may learn something about himself.

- Look beneath the surface. If you notice that your spouse takes every opportunity to regale new victims with her story of meeting a movie star or driving cross-country alone, consider the vulnerabilities that lie underneath this constant retelling. Does she feel insecure and think meeting George Clooney makes her seem more desirable? Ask her what she thinks this story conveys to other people. Seeing your partner's vulnerabilities can enable you to approach her with more empathy.

- Focus on your partner's interest—even if you find it dull—for five minutes with open curiosity. Actively inquire about his golf, Xbox, or upcoming camping trip. Pick up the book or magazine he's just finished and take a look. Your voluntary attention will likely be perceived as an act of generosity. Bonus: By overcoming your reactive disinterest, you may actually learn something—about the subject or about your spouse.

- Watch your spouse's body language for signs of indifference. Is he yawning, averting his eyes, surreptitiously watching TV in the mirror behind you? Either inquire why you've lost him, or change the subject. Keep in mind that it could be you are broaching an entirely foreign topic that in some way overwhelms your spouse and that his yawn is the reflexive response to exposure to something very different. Perhaps you're monopolizing the conversation. It may be there is no way he is ever going to join in your passion or show curiosity for scrap booking. Accept this disconnect and instead call a friend who shares your mutual interest.

Chapter 14

The Complication
of Compliments

Offering daily compliments infuses a marriage with warmth. This positive feedback can be anything from "You look beautiful in that dress, and it makes me proud to be your husband," to "When you gave that man five dollars it inspired me to be kind to strangers as well." A simple compliment ("You are nice") offers a greater possibility of connection if you comment on what you find pleasing and then follow up with how this observation made you feel ("You are generous and that makes me feel safe"). The same happens when you thank your partner and follow it up with: "It makes me feel seen/appreciated/respected/ loved," etc. When you do this, you enhance your feedback with an even more personal level of mutual understanding. Taking five minutes each day to confer a positive message onto a loved one shines a ray of light into your partner's life.

Who Benefits?

Compliments are really about kindness; they just make people feel good. Psychological research backs up the feel-good nature of giving compliments. Sonja Lyubomirsky, Professor of Psychology at the University of California, conducted a study to answer the age-old question: Do happier people perform more acts of kindness or does kindness make people happier? She divided randomly selected subjects into two groups and then asked one group to engage in an act of kindness, but not the second group. Her results support the idea that benevolence promotes happiness but not vice-versa; the group who performed the kind act showed at least a temporary increase in their subjective feelings of well-being compared to those who were not asked to engage.

SAY THIS

"I don't tell you enough how wonderful you are. I appreciate everything you do for me."

So is positive feedback advantageous for you or for your partner? It's beneficial for both. A sense of personal empowerment follows when you offer another person a humane gesture. If you're not sure how to give this type of constructive feedback or aren't sure what areas of your partner's life to focus on, try these options:

- **Appearance**: Attractiveness, weight loss/gain, new hair, clothing choice, or healthy looking skin.
- **Daily Actions**: Being kind, smart, funny, generous, or supportive.
- **Work Life**: Being determined, focused, strategic, or ambitious.
- **Creativity**: Finding an interesting solution, making your home beautiful, writing a terrific letter/article, or following an artistic passion.

These ideas are just a start. Take five minutes today and think about what draws you to your spouse. What initially attracted you? What surprising developments enhance your togetherness? Then, choose a moment to express your thoughts and watch how good you feel. It's likely your partner will also beam with gratitude.

You can also take five minutes to write down your emotions. For some, it can be easier to be open and vulnerable on paper. If you're shy or self-conscious about giving compliments this strategy might be more comfortable for you. Letters, notes, or even e-mails can be precious reminders of your love.

When Giving Compliments Doesn't Come Naturally

For some, giving compliments—even to a cherished loved one—doesn't come easily. This may be the result of a childhood where love and generosity were shown through actions, not words. It may also be tied in to your or your spouse's culture. America's culture tends to be more open in the area of giving and receiving compliments than other cultures that may feel such displays of emotion are excessive and perhaps disingenuous. However even in American culture there are many who believe that over-praising can encourage arrogance rather than humility. This fear of pride doesn't promote long-term warmth in a marriage. If you have something positive to say about your partner, overcome your resistance and say it. People who hear an affirmation about themselves will generally strive to live up to it instead of resting on their laurels.

Finally, for some, giving compliments risks awkwardness or vulnerability; you may be embarrassed for your partner to know how much you really care about him. You may feel that your spouse will have the upper hand in your relationship if you express your admiration. You may feel that you need to play a game of disinterest to keep your partner from becoming complacent, taking you for granted, and eventually leaving. This strategy is not a wholesome way to approach another person and it doesn't promote happiness. Instead, state your positive feelings from a position of independence: "I love you, admire you, and respect you." (Then think to yourself: "But I also feel that way about myself.") Or, "You are a great catch." ("And so am I.") Giving these compliments to yourself is the best antidote to the fear of a loss of power by showing your hand.

Extra Credit

Another way to make your spouse's eyes shine is to compliment someone or something you know he loves, whether a family member, restaurant, or band. For example, "Hey, you know, I was listening to so-and-so's new album, and you're right, they are amazing!" or "I just love your mother. She's hilarious."

The next time you notice yourself hesitant to praise your spouse, take five minutes to explore why. Are you unaccustomed to giving compliments? Do you fear your partner will change in a negative way, becoming arrogant, perhaps? Or, worse, is there a worry that you will be left behind once she realizes what a prize she is? Take all of this resistance and throw it out the window. Then, choose a quality that inspires you and yell it from the rooftops. (Or tell her over dinner. Or slip her a note. Or whisper it in her ear.)

Receiving a Compliment

For many people, it is more challenging to receive a compliment than it is to give one. Imagine someone asks if you have lost weight. Do you demur and say, "No, these jeans are just really flattering?" Or your spouse brags to his friends that you are a genius cook and you blush. Later, you say to him how much pressure that puts on you: "No one is going to want to invite us over for a meal." Does your partner ooze confidence that your money worries will be over soon because you are "such a smart businessman"? Deep down, perhaps you don't agree and feel like a fraud.

SAY THIS
"You may not believe what an inspiration you are, but I'm going to keep telling you anyway. You make me want to strive to be a better person. Thank you."

If you feel you cannot live up to your spouse's praise, you don't have to. Live up to your own best version of yourself. Study your own moral code. Understand what you believe is right and what you feel is wrong. Then follow your standard and you will feel happy, as will your lucky partner.

Keep Complimenting
When you give a compliment and it's received with self-consciousness and vulnerability, should you decide that the kindest act is to keep your admiration to yourself? The answer is no. Positive affirmations offered to a loved one are the fodder for continuing warmth between two people. The more you praise your partner, the more he'll ultimately feel good about himself and good about you. Besides, it is in the best

interest of the receiver to accept the compliment in the spirit in which it is given. Perhaps there is exaggeration, but so what? It inspires the one giving the compliment to match the excellence she perceives in you.

SARAH & JASON'S STORY

Sarah was used to compliments. In fact, in their absence, she felt something must be amiss. And, after ten years of marriage to Jason, who rarely praised her, she began to assume he just didn't find her all that pretty or smart. She brought it up a few times, but it was a difficult problem to voice without sounding conceited or needy. So, she kept her feelings under wraps.

The issue came to a head when Sarah began a friendship with a man at work who clearly—and vocally—admired her. At first, their lunches were innocent, but as the months passed, she felt her attachment to Henry was becoming too intimate. Sarah loved that he noticed her carefully chosen outfits and complimented her quick mind. It reminded her of the supportive environment in which she grew up.

Before it went any further, she felt compelled to discuss the situation with Jason, whom she loved deeply. Over coffee one morning, she took a deep breath and began: "As you know, I've been spending a lot of time with Henry. Before you get worried, nothing is happening between us. But, our friendship has made me realize something that I feel is missing in our marriage: you rarely compliment me. Henry does, and the contrast is striking. I feel happy and confident around him."

"You know you're beautiful. You're obviously smart to have the job you have. So, why do you need me to repeat these things?"

"Because I feel unnoticed by you. Don't you enjoy it when I tell you that you look handsome?"

"Frankly, it makes me uncomfortable. It's too much."

"Well, I'm going to continue to tell you because it's true and I would appreciate you considering this need of mine going forward."

"I will keep it in mind. . . . Gorgeous."

Jason was unused to giving compliments. His parents were more inclined to point out his flaws than his successes. As an adult, he didn't believe he had many qualities worth praising. Sarah's insistence that he was worthy of her love just made him uncomfortable; it made him feel like a fraud. Why would he want her to feel the same way? Their five-minute conversation was Sarah's first step toward showing Jason that she needed exactly what he found difficult to hear. He'll have to take her at her word and overcome his resistance. Once Sarah and Jason become accustomed to the act of complimenting one another, each will live their lives with more confidence.

The more centered and comfortable you are with yourself, the more at ease you will feel giving—and receiving—compliments. Make an effort to infuse your marriage with this simple (yet surprisingly complex!) act. Remember: We all derive happiness from giving pleasure to others. Praising your spouse is actually a gift to yourself.

Why is giving compliments so complicated? When you are in a loving relationship, shouldn't it be natural to continually tell each other how wonderful you are? For some people, yes, but for many, compliments fall by the wayside or become fraught with self-consciousness or shame. When you are first dating, it feels right to admire her eyes or his sexiness, but, over time, is it really necessary to keep up with all that flattery? Yes. In five minutes a day you have the power to alter your lover's self-perception for the better. It is a gift that costs nothing, but can mean everything. Plus, it provides you, the giver, with a feeling of well-being and joy.

- It only takes a few minutes to express your admiration for your spouse. Tell him he's sexy when you first wake up to give his day a boost. Or, at the end of the day, recall something he did that you admire and discuss it over dinner. For example, "I loved watching you play with the kids this afternoon. You are such a great father." If you make this a daily or weekly exercise, your mate will likely strive to live up to your words of praise.
- Write a brief letter or e-mail to your loved one explaining what you admire about her. Then, leave it on her dresser—or in her inbox—for her to smile about later. You don't have to write a novel; even a simple "I love you" can make someone's day.
- Make it public. Giving your spouse an appropriate compliment in the presence of certain individuals can influence how they see him. If you have his boss over for dinner, slip in that he scored in the top 10 per-

cent on the GRE. If his mother insists he's not cut out to be a father, choose an appropriate moment to brag about the sacrifices he's making for your kids. Take on the role of proud, indulgent spouse, but if you suspect public praise may make him uncomfortable, it's wise to let him know in advance what you are planning to say.

- If you have difficulty giving compliments, spend five minutes meditating on why this is. Personal history? The risk of vulnerability? Then, tell yourself these feelings don't have to control your behavior and commit to saying something kind to your spouse today. If you fear embarrassment, remember compliments can take many forms. It doesn't have to be poetry. Start off with admiring the meal she made or how he handled the car on those wet roads.

- Does receiving compliments make you uncomfortable? Spend a few minutes considering why this is. Did your parents ever take the time to praise you? Then, the next time your partner admires your figure or your ability to balance the checkbook, don't demur. Just say, "Thanks, I am trying hard to believe what you see in me." Your spouse loves you for all your great qualities. If you start to believe it, you can approach your marriage with more confidence.

Chapter 15

The Benefits of Giving— and Taking—Space

You married your spouse hoping to be together forever. But, how do you define togetherness? Is it constant companionship, being connected at the emotional hip all day every day? Or is it a loose camaraderie, with room to breathe and grow independent from one another? Everyone has different space needs, but the latter option is the more expansive. Giving your partner autonomy—and taking some for yourself—means carving out separate places that allow each of you to step away, even if for just a short time daily. It also means encouraging each other to pursue personal passions, even if hockey is not your game, or hitting the flea market on Saturdays makes him cringe.

Merging with another (commonly called being co-dependent) can interfere with personal discovery, and this self-deadening glue can chip away at the strongest marriage. Finding the balance between being together but separate stimulates vitality and interest for both partners.

Autonomy Clears the Air

Close contact can cause strain. As much as you love your spouse, conflict is inevitable, especially if you have children. In a marriage there are two types of struggles that can cause stress. One is a voluntary effort, if one partner wants something before the other one thinks of it. The one who desires change must face the slower partner's initial resistance to join what is desired. For example, if one of you wants another child or wants to move to a new city, a serious debate may be in store.

The second type of struggle is one that is imposed involuntarily by an outside event. This could be a job change, illness, or even something positive: "I got a raise! How do you think we should spend the money?" In either type of discord, when tension becomes too intense, time away can lower the fire. Taking a break from the discussion or argument—even for only five minutes—clears your mind until a new way of looking at the dilemma begins to appear.

SAY THIS

"Okay, obviously we are not seeing eye-to-eye on this. Before things get too heated, I'd like to take a break. Let me make a sandwich (for both of us, if you'd like), then let's continue the discussion."

Walking away or giving your partner some alone time allows the pressure to dissipate; you both receive the time to let go of the stressor point that's causing the pressure in the first place. In a marriage, private time and space clears the mind to become a more creative collaborator in every aspect of togetherness.

Try one of these activities to clear your mind:

- **Exercise**: Walking or jogging around the block gets your blood pumping. It's simple, effective, and is a great stress-reliever.
- **Creativity**: Try artistic expression. Go put the finishing touches on that painting or complete that sweater you've been knitting.
- **Self-Care**: Take a shower or bath. The warm water will soothe your churning mind.
- **Music**: Listen to music. Often, good music can break your mind open to new thoughts.
- **Meditation and Prayer**: Meditate or engage in traditional prayer. Reaching deep into yourself or to a higher power can put your daily struggles into perspective.

The Biology of Taking Five

When you walk away and take a break, you'll return better able to see, hear, listen, think, and function. The calmness you feel after taking a break is physically traced to the release of nitric oxide throughout the body, countering the negative effects of the fight or flight hormones related to the stress response. When you find yourself in a marital conflict, secretions such as adrenaline, norepinephrine (noradrenaline), and cortisol flood your system. Your blood vessels constrict, causing a racing heart, high blood pressure, anger, anxiety, and greater vulnerability to pain. These secretions raise your body to an elevated level of readiness, a state that was essential for hunter-gathers to guard against predators, as well as in present time for top-level performance. After a certain point, however, those stress hormones become counter-productive. Like a record skipping, your mind gets stuck in an unproductive loop.

The most effective way to get unstuck is to walk away for a few minutes. As you take a walk or make a pot of tea, your brain releases calming neurotransmitters such as dopamine (linked to feelings of well-being and happiness) and endorphins (morphine-like secretions that lead to soothing and the reduction of pain). As a result, your blood vessels open up, your heart rate decreases, stress fades, and inner tranquility emerges.

ANTHONY & HALLIE'S STORY

Whenever Hallie addressed a conflict, her husband Anthony immediately became defensive. For Hallie, this was frustrating as she felt she could rarely speak a full sentence before Anthony burst in to tell his side of it. She would shout over his defense, "Let me speak, let me speak!"

After being exposed to the way they argue, I suggested that when the stress reached such a peak, one of them should go for a brief walk. Anthony always felt that he was not permitted to leave when the tension got high because Hallie assumed he was threatening to leave permanently instead of just taking a break. They devised the following strategy: Whenever the conversation became heated, Hallie would change the subject to something collaborative: their toddler or new business venture. Often this calmed down Anthony's defensiveness and soothed Hallie, alleviating her fear that he would leave her.

One evening, Hallie paused their argument about how long her in-laws should visit. "Let's revisit this in a moment. I was thinking about our business plan this morning. Don't you agree we should approach investors before the holidays?"

"That's a great idea, Hallie. I'm excited about pitching our idea. I want to talk more about having my parents come up, but will you excuse me while I go to the store for a soda?"

"Sure. I'll be here when you get back."

Hallie and Anthony devised a strategy that worked for them. Anthony's defensiveness was curtailed and Hallie's fear of abandonment was bypassed. When you find it difficult to offer your partner autonomy, remind yourself that the gift of space, even for just a few minutes, is often all that is needed to break the negative thought patterns that hinder connection.

The Pursuit of Happiness

You and your spouse are unlikely to share every interest. This is not only okay, but also necessary to stay mutually intrigued. One study from the *Journal of Marital and Family Therapy* explored the connection between autonomy and relatedness in 141 married couples. "Autonomy was measured by evaluating spouses' perceptions of the extent to which partners encouraged a sense of independence and individuality for the spouses. Relatedness was measured by evaluating spouses' perceptions of the amount of closeness that partners provided. It was found that autonomy and relatedness were significantly positively correlated with each other, as well as with marital adjustment for both males and females."

Extra Credit

Demonstrate your love to your partner by asking her to take five minutes to teach you about a particular interest—preferably one you assume is beyond boring. You may not care about gardening, but the connection created by standing side by side, your hands in the earth, is real.

Maybe you like novels, but he enjoys video games. Or, you'll never understand why she *must* see the latest Jennifer Aniston romantic comedy. Offering open-minded, guilt-free autonomy to each other so you can pursue the things that make you happy is generous. Follow up your offer of independence with genuine curiosity. Maybe you couldn't care less about baseball, but being inquisitive about the Red Sox for a few minutes shows your partner that you care about *him*. Give him space to watch his game, and then remind yourself to take five minutes to ask about the final score, his favorite play, or who he predicts will win the World Series.

Too Much Autonomy?

Space in a long-term partnership is crucial. But, what if one spouse is comfortable spending weeks apart while the other would be fine separating for an afternoon now and again? Someone who enjoys a great deal of autonomy risks his partner feeling abandoned or isolated. If you know this about yourself or your spouse, your space mismatch requires a daily calibration. It only takes a few minutes to check in with your partner to see if more or less space is desired. A compromise may be required: If you want to go deep-sea fishing in the Caribbean for a week, but your wife feels that's too much time away, offer instead to go to a U.S. coast for a long weekend. She may still wish you were staying home, but you both are making an effort to find middle ground.

SAY THIS
. . . .
"I want to you be able to follow your dream, but can we find a way to make it more comfortable for me? A week (or weekend) away feels better than a month."

As in dance, distance prevents you and your partner from stepping on each other's toes. It allows love to flow. Another apt analogy for autonomy in a marriage is that it's the space that allows oxygen in to create a roaring, warming fire.

Five-Minute Strategies

Whether it's five minutes, an hour, or a week, taking time away to explore independent interests and satisfying idiosyncratic needs offers renewed energy in a marriage. Self-sufficiency is an inoculation against stultifying obligations. Use five minutes of autonomy as a tool when you are faced with a moment of conflict. Or, take five minutes to explain to your partner why you need space to pursue your individual passion. The challenge of achieving happy autonomy in your marriage is agreeing—or compromising—on the appropriate amount of independence from one another. Keep in mind that too much togetherness can prevent you both from blossoming into your full potential as individuals.

- Request a five-minute breather during a conflict, then go on a walk, get a glass of water, or do some housework. Use stepping away during an argument as an attempt to break your own defensiveness and negative thought patterns. Time alone allows both you and your partner to think creatively about the problem and reapproach it with a fresh perspective.
- Take freedom to pursue outside interests. Then, for just a few minutes, invite your partner to share your hobby or passion. This could mean telling her the score of the game or recounting what was said at your book club. Your spouse doesn't have to share your interest, but may learn something new.
- Take a few minutes to inquire about your partner's outside interests. As we discussed in Chapter 13, you never know what the other is thinking and you may

discover a new angle to this person you have known for so long. Your interest will give your partner confidence that her independent efforts are something you admire and accept.

- If you crave companionship at all times, begin your stretch for autonomy by taking daily five-minute breathers. Instead of joining your wife for coffee in the morning, take the dog out early with a to-go cup and enjoy your alone time. Or, let your husband go to bed first while you send out a few e-mails. These small steps are valuable and will be the beginning of letting some air into your marriage.

- If you spend most of your time pursuing your individual interests and your spouse feels neglected, think of a few ways you can include her. For example, if you spend every Saturday in the park playing chess, invite her to meet you for a picnic in between games. Introduce her around so she knows all your chess buddies. Small efforts of inclusion can go far in mending a heart that's hurting. Hold on to your autonomy, but be sure to carve out a space for togetherness.

- Invite your other half to find a middle ground if you have different space needs. A short conversation explaining how you desire more or less time together will hopefully invite compromise. Allow time to process this introductory idea. Revisit it briefly from time to time until you find some middle ground.

Chapter 16

Compassionate Feedback

In his play *No Exit*, Jean-Paul Sartre shows us that living in close quarters with others can be hell on earth. So why do it? The most obvious reason is companionship. But, after the initial thrill of falling in love fades, a crucial role of mates is to become witnesses to one another's existence. You have a one-of-a-kind expertise for observing and supporting your spouse's growth—or lack thereof. After all, who knows a person better than his other half?

Imagine an ideal partnership as two strong people creating an upside down V. Think of the power that can be generated by leaning against one another. When you're off base, your significant other will help set you straight, and vice-versa. This feedback mechanism defines the essence of a fertile marriage. Devoid of this advantage, you lose out on a valuable tool for living a progressively creative, full life.

Safety in Love

After many years together, your reaction to your partner's viewpoint depends on a variety of factors: tone, subject matter, and most importantly how safe you feel in the relationship. Dr. Diana Fosha, a psychologist on the faculty at New

York University, maintains that compassionate feedback substitutes "radical challenge and pressure (for) radical empathy and emotional engagement through attunement, resonance, affect sharing affirmation and self-disclosure. Through the support of an emotionally engaged (other), the terrors of love, affirmation, and feeling good (can) truly be discerned."

When partners feel supported and safe, optimal functioning and a feeling of well-being is possible. On the other hand, the expression of intense emotions without the security of feeling loved is toxic. If you don't feel that your spouse is on your side, you'll naturally develop defenses or self-protection against open emotional interchanges. You'll consider any feedback to be destructive, and your evolution as a couple will go awry. For example, imagine you say to your wife in a perfectly neutral tone: "I wish you would rinse the dishes before you put them in the dishwasher." Her reaction could go one of two ways. The one who feels safe and loved in the marriage may respond: "Sure, no problem." The partner who lacks that security may lash out in defensiveness, "You are so critical! Load them yourself."

The more you feel that your partner understands you, the more you'll be able to accept feedback from him. On the other hand, if the space between you is uncomfortable or is filled with tension, there is less likelihood for constructive dialogue. In *Handbook of Attachment: Theory, Research and Clinical Applications*, a classic compendium of attachment theory, contributor Mary Main writes, "The roots of resilience and the capacity to withstand emotionally aversive situations without resorting to defensive exclusion are to be found in the sense of being understood by and existing in the mind and heart of a loving, attuned, and self-possessed other."

Resisting Criticism

There is a distinction between giving compassionate feedback and being critical. You know it when you feel it. Tone, body language, and word choice can make the difference between a constructive or destructive interaction as you can see in the table below.

Criticism	Compassionate Feedback
"Ugh—your breath!"	"Did you brush your teeth today? I know I sometimes forget."
"You are driving like a maniac."	"Are you stressed about time? You don't usually go over the speed limit."
"Way to charm my parents. I don't think you said two words at dinner."	"I noticed you were quiet tonight. Do you feel okay?"
"Those fries will go straight to your thighs."	"Let's share those fries and split a salad for our entrée."

Addressing undesirable behavior in your partner with derision or sarcasm will not foster receptivity. The next time you want to offer feedback, take a five-minute breather to consider the best way to approach the situation. If his behavior has been annoying you for months, resist attack. Take a few deep breaths and consider how to approach the problem with empathy. You may even want to grab a pen and paper and write down a script that will prevent you from devolving into criticism. Start with something affirming, such as: "I love the way you tell stories. You use so much detail that they really come to life. But sometimes with all that specificity you lose me, and perhaps Jerry felt that way at dinner last night. Could we develop a signal so that when I feel lost, you'll resist going off on a tangent?"

More Than Words

There are many five-minute, nonverbal behaviors to demonstrate compassionate feedback that can positively persuade your spouse. Living by example is a powerful way to influence change. If you stop drinking after one glass of wine, your partner is unlikely to feel comfortable ordering another bottle. Bringing in a third-party expert is also a great way to support your desires. Wish she would floss more? Bring home a pamphlet from the dentist that discusses the risks of not doing so. These quick, oblique strategies for offering feedback carry less risk of immediate resistance.

The Downside of Bottling It Up

It can sometimes be tempting to keep feathers unruffled and avoid offering constructive feedback. After all, being authentic about how your spouse's behavior affects you may invite conflict. You could just keep quiet about your view of your husband's career passivity and how it makes you feel defeated, or how you feel fear and anger when your wife speaks harshly to your kids. Staying mute may allay conflict, but it also invites disconnect over time.

Mutual understanding is earned by facing experiences as they transpire and not allowing them to go underground or escalate to disruptive intensity. Observing you gritting your teeth when your mate lets another work opportunity pass him by ensures that he'll feel your diminishing respect, but not understand why. Wouldn't a five-minute offer of open-minded feedback be the better choice? Consider the following conversation:

"I noticed you let that potential client's call go straight to voicemail. I know it's a Saturday, but what are your thoughts about work opportunities that pop up?"

"Aw, come on. I'll call the guy back on Monday morning."

"Do you believe you deserve success?"

"Definitely."

"Are you at all concerned about the competition?"

"Not really, I know I am good at what I do."

"Sure, but the next person he calls could answer the phone and get the job."

"You're right. I'll call him back after the game."

Feedback offered with curiosity, like this example, may result in your partner immediately agreeing with you, but it's possible that your spouse could resist or ignore you. Develop an atmosphere where your other half wants to hear your opinion. Usually unsolicited advice is not welcome and is experienced as a boundary violation, but when there is comfortable space, freedom is encouraged and judgment is minimized. In this environment, the power to sway behavior over time increases.

If you have feedback for your partner, find out first if he is open to it or if he would rather figure things out for himself. If the second option is his choice, your role is then to create an atmosphere where you become a nonjudgmental sounding board. This is difficult but not impossible to achieve if you are able to visualize this stance. Picturing it happening can make it actually happen over time. Keep in mind: When you offer your observation of the other person, always add how your observation makes you feel either about him or about yourself. This increases connection.

EVAN & BARBARA'S STORY

A few months ago Evan went on a business trip to Europe. His wife Barbara accompanied him. During the trip, Evan felt that Barbara came across as too flirty, too seductive toward his colleagues. Yet, he never gave her any feedback as to how uncomfortable her clothing and her joking made him feel in front of these people. When they returned home there was a strained silence between them. Evan planned to take the next trip to South America without Barbara. She was hurt and rejected and clueless as to why this rift had occurred. From Evan's point of view, he felt the need for self-protection and resisted intimacy and closeness with Barbara.

He struggled with figuring out how to express himself and resume a closer connection with Barbara. Evan was concerned that his attempt to give feedback to her would be met with derision, rejection, or humiliation. These fears led to loss, a feeling of abuse, and self-annihilation. Barbara felt left out and Evan was lonely.

What were the benefits of approaching Barbara?

Hopefully with real contact Evan could regain a feeling of safety and pleasure with Barbara and rightful ownership of his own thoughts and emotions. Taking a leap, he began, "Barbara, you may have noticed that we have not been talking much lately. Something is on my mind about our trip to Europe that I finally have the courage to discuss."

"Yes, I noticed we've been distant and I really want to hear what's going on."

"I felt that on the trip you were dressed too seductively and also behaved too friendly toward my colleagues. It embarrassed me."

"Wow, thanks for the feedback. From my point of view, I'm just a soccer mom and had no idea how you wanted me to dress. I was just trying to be friendly."

"Thank you for listening and not being insulted."

"So can I come with you on the next trip?"

"I'll think about it. I feel more energized and hopeful now that this is out in the open."

By taking a risk and telling Barbara what the disconnect was all about, Evan increased his empathy for her as well as for himself. According to psychologist Diana Fosha, the straight back and forth of truth involves the capacity "to express feelings directly to the person . . . to remain connected taking in the other's reaction, and to sustain this emotional conversation through time." Many emotions are tapped into following their discussion, such as: feeling moved, touched, or strongly aroused within oneself, and feeling gratitude, love, tenderness, and appreciation toward the other.

The aim of creating an optimum feeling of safety is to provide a forum for each person to be able to give and receive helpful feedback which can be used as fuel for developing innate potential and can also be used to access real emotions for self healing. The ideal is to provide a secure grounding so that you or your partner can abandon any survival defense mechanisms that developed when you were younger and felt less supported. Now, as adults, new growth for both of you can take place over a lifetime of fertile feedback.

It is helpful to consider the Golden Rule when offering feedback: Treat others as you would like to be treated. How would you like your partner to approach *you* when he feels your behavior could use some tweaks? A soft touch is usually best—and garners the most results. Using a five-minute model to offer constructive feedback can help you take a thoughtful, empathetic approach rather than overwhelming and/or trapping your partner with too much information over a discussion that goes on for too long.

- Pause before you engage. How are your tone and choice of words likely to be received? It may be tempting to use harsh words or sarcasm—especially if the issue at hand is particularly maddening. Resist. Take a few minutes to write out a kinder way to approach the problem. Talk about your own struggles with the issue first in order to create an even playing field and minimize defensiveness.
- Offer feedback with curiosity. Instead of pointing out the reasons you feel a particular behavior may be interfering with your partner's goal, ask why the behavior happens in the first place. This also lessens the chance of your partner closing the door with a defensive response. Keep in mind that you don't want to make assumptions about your partner. Ask questions with an open mind and you may be surprised by the answer.
- Look for ways to give feedback without saying a word. In five minutes, you could model how you wish the other person would behave (cleaning up after dinner, speaking respectfully to the waiter). Over time, this type of modeling can influence your partner's behavior. The benefit

here is that under-the-radar feedback limits conflict. After all, you've said nothing about your spouse's typical rudeness to waiters, per se. But when he sees you happily bantering with your server, not to mention the good service you receive, he may consider changing his behavior.

- Stop by your doctor's office to grab a pamphlet about the importance of getting annual checkups; swing by the bookstore to buy a book on how to handle grief. Enlisting third party experts can help you make your case and stop comments like "Oh, what do you know?" and "Who are you to tell me__?" in their tracks. Keep in mind: Stick to the experts. Enlisting your partner's mother, coworker, or other intimate friend may make him feel ganged up on.

- Even if you tend to be conflict-adverse, don't keep your thoughts to yourself. Bottling up your frustration over your partner's behavior will only cause a disconnect between the two of you over time. Although it can be difficult in the short run, one of the great advantages of long-term partnerships is our ability to witness and support each other's growth. Engage in a five-minute conversation that compassionately outlines your hopes for yourself and your goodwill toward your partner.

- Are you on the receiving end of constructive feedback? Resist becoming defensive or shutting out your other half in anger. Offer your spouse five minutes to make his case. Tell him you are willing to be open-minded about the issue at hand and are sure he has both of your best interests at heart. Even if you still don't agree with your spouse at the end of the five minutes, or after you've had time to digest his thoughts, listening with an open heart fosters trust and mutual respect. Plus, he will be more willing to listen to you when the tables are turned.

PART 4

Five-Minute Strategies for Marital Hiccups

Chapter 17

Tuning in with Emotional Intelligence

Communicating empathically with others is an idea popularized by Daniel Goleman in his book, *Emotional Intelligence*. Approaching your marriage with emotional intelligence means tuning into your own palette of feelings, as well as heightening your awareness of your spouse's inner reality. Resilience and well-being emerge as you integrate your energy and information with that of your partner.

Of course, this is often easier said than done. We all would like to know what's below the surface—especially during a conflict. But our own disturbing mysteries, hair-trigger anger, and defensiveness can drown us before we calm down enough to tune into our spouse's angst. In addition, those of us who experienced a childhood lacking in secure bonds with our caregivers may never have learned how to tune into another person.

Luckily, as with any other skill, you can acquire emotional intelligence with practice. Choosing to concentrate on your expressive life for just a few minutes a day will lead to a new language—a new way of knowing your own inner self as well as your partner's. This is the basis for building a stronger bond with your spouse.

The Biology of Emotion

Emotions are nonconscious mental processes. They prepare us for action. Within the brain the *amygdala*, a cluster of neurons, acts as a receiving and sending station between input from the outer world and your emotions. As a coordinating center the amygdala—which is especially sensitive to social interactions—plays a crucial role in integrating your immediate perceptions of reality with all of your stored memories; the combination of your perceptions and memories influences how you behave.

Since the sensations of the mind are wordless and exist without consciousness, tuning in to what is going on inside your own brain before you try to figure out what's going on in your spouse's is essential for knowing how to approach a conflict. Primary emotions—anger, fear, sadness, and joy—directly mirror changes in states of mind. Recognizing these in yourself and in your spouse creates a feeling of belonging. A 2001 research project published in the Journal of Social Psychology examined the link between emotional intelligence and interpersonal relations among diverse age groups in the United States. They discovered the higher participants rated their partners for emotional intelligence, the higher their marital satisfaction and the more they anticipated greater satisfaction in their relationships.

Emotional Self-Regulation

In his book, *The Mindful Brain,* neurobiologist Daniel J. Siegel discusses how our original attachments to other people create the foundation for a coherent sense of self. The more stable your foundation and the more stable you feel, the more open you'll be to tuning into your partner. In a secure attachment with original caregivers, the signals of one person are directly responded to by the other. This is the tool that will help you know when to walk away from a conflict and when to stay and face it.

If your amygdala is excessively sensitive and fires off a "Danger!" signal, it will automatically alter your perceptions, and it will appear as if something threatening is happening. In a relationship, you may begin a disagreement with your partner that is completely within your own brain. Most of us can relate to the experience of conducting an entire argument in our own heads. You walk around muttering, tweaking the script of what you'll say and how he'll likely respond. Learn to read and control these internal outbursts so when you feel the danger signal you'll know whether to approach your partner or take a walk around the block. Discovering how to read your own preconscious emotions and not act them out goes a long way to maintaining a happy long-term relationship.

Emotional regulation allows the mind to be flexible. The capacity to reflect on your mental state and to integrate this knowledge is key to understanding the minds of others. Without such self-awareness, you become a prisoner of your own instability. You can train yourself to know when you are close to the edge or already flooded. Here are several five-minute techniques you can use to talk yourself off the proverbial cliff:

Deep Breathing
Meditation
Repetitive Actions
Singing
Laughing

Employ the best personal tool to bring your intellect back in control of your emotions. This way, you can use your emotional intelligence to make a rational choice during a conflict, rather than impulsively acting with no positive end goal in mind.

Tuning Into Your Partner

Once you've deciphered your own emotions, it's time to turn your attention to your partner. The first step toward attunement is realizing that, like art, people can be engaging or opaque, depending on your own perception. They are constantly transforming, shifting underneath the surface. What a wonderful challenge!

Extra Credit

Imagine that your spouse's emotional life is an iceberg, with just the tip within view. The majority of her feelings and sensations exist out of sight, beneath the waves. Conjure up this image for five minutes a day and appreciate the awesome challenge of truly knowing another soul.

Emotionally intelligent people tend to rely on benevolence and compassion to connect to others. Even when your partner is behaving in a (to you) negative manner, try to access your empathy to see the child within who is acting out because he is, perhaps, frightened or lonely. If your partner senses your willingness to put yourself in his shoes, he is more likely to open up and admit that he snapped at you because he is preoccupied with worry over layoffs at his company. Or, maybe he was quiet at dinner because the host embarrassed him with that comment about his moustache.

Some people reveal themselves more easily than others. So what are several quick, five-minute strategies that can optimize your chances of accurately tuning into your partner, even if she tends to be reticent? First, do your homework. What is happening in your spouse's life that could be affecting her well-being? Is she happy because she feels good about losing ten pounds? Is she miserable because she doesn't feel attractive but is pretending everything is fine? Is she obviously fed up, making everyone in your household unhappy as well? Why? Pay close attention to passing expressions (is her smile open or a bit brittle?), comments, what clothes she chooses, what she's eating (you know she only eats cake when she's upset). Conduct your research as if you were an anthropologist, studying what makes her tick.

The other option is to just go ahead and ask how your spouse is feeling. But be open and honest about yourself first. This will create an equal playing field.

SAY THIS

"I've been down ever since the holidays. I don't know if it's the long, dark days, or if my job is getting to me. How are you these days?"

Often, people sense that something is going on inside themselves, yet are unsure what or why. Fortunately, you can help your spouse explore her personal terrain. Start off slowly—five minutes here and there is a good beginning. Avoid overwhelming her with unsolicited observations or suffocating heart-to-hearts. Tuning in means recognizing when your partner is receptive to discussion, and when quiet companionship is preferable.

You can also use humor to shine a light on your partner's mind and heart. Of course, this is specific for each couple as it is highly subjective. But, imagine your spouse has been unusually crabby for the past week. If you outright ask what's going on, you may be turned away with a curt, "Nothing. What's going on with *you?*" Engage in your own style of light-hearted fun to get to the root of the problem. Perhaps come home with a balloon on which you've drawn a frowny face. Tie it to a chair at dinner, and for five minutes, pretend it's your spouse, while ignoring your actual partner's pleas for a return to sanity. Once she catches on, surely a smile will be forthcoming and, hopefully, a chink in her emotional armor.

HARRY & NANCY'S STORY

It was Thanksgiving, and Harry and Nancy were looking forward to ending what had been a stressful evening with Nancy's mother, Joan. As usual, Joan had had too much to drink and was raging about the misdeeds of her ex-husband, Nancy's father. "You know, Nancy, he told me once your sister was his favorite. Something about Ann being the brighter of you two." With that, Nancy and Harry said their goodbyes and fled.

Weeks later, Harry began to notice that Nancy was a bit moodier than usual. She was using more sarcasm, and laughing less often. It was subtle, but it had begun to bother him. One evening, he decided to explore what was going on.

"Nancy, I feel like we haven't spent quality time together recently. I miss you. Fill me in on how you're doing."

"I'm good. Didn't we just spend this entire weekend together?"

"We did, we did. But part of me still feels like the old Nancy has gone into hiding. Are you sure you're okay? You seem sad."

At this, Nancy burst into tears. "You know me so well. I can't hide anything from you. I thought it would pass, but my mom's comment at Thanksgiving has been festering. I don't know how to process the fact that my dad said such an awful thing. How could he?"

"Well, he probably didn't. You know your mom can't stand that you have a relationship with him and likes to cause trouble. If you need to know, why don't you ask him? It would probably be a huge relief."

"You're right. I need to deal with this and move on."

Harry's inquiries into his wife's emotional state were steeped in compassion. This allowed Nancy to feel secure enough to open up and describe her truth. Before this conversation, Nancy hadn't put words to how bereft she felt. She was swimming in pure emotion. With Harry's help, she gave words to her feelings, which in turn gave her the power to confront the problem and resume living her happy life.

Tuning into your partner takes empathy and patience, but with both you can come to appreciate and identify with this person you chose for life. It's a never-ending, but rewarding journey that will fortify your love.

Five-Minute Strategies

Tuning in to yourself and your spouse means not being the victim of your emotional lives. Imagine a small child throwing a tantrum. He doesn't have the capacity to understand why he can't have a piece of candy or a toy, but you do and you can use your emotions as a divining rod to discern what behavior will garner the most happiness. Through emotional intelligence, you can help your spouse (and vice-versa) access her expressive life, use what she needs, and discard the rest. This doesn't happen overnight. But every day, five-minute explorations of you and your partner's realities will gradually increase your ability to tune in.

- Adjust to your authenticity. For five minutes a day—especially when you feel flooded by anger, fear, or sadness—choose an activity that you find relaxing, such as deep breathing or exercise. Explore what your emotions are telling you and then respond accordingly. Perhaps you're embarrassed that you didn't get the promotion. Understanding this, you can use the pain as motivation to work harder, rather than mope or pick a fight with your spouse.
- Become an anthropologist. Take a few minutes a day to clue yourself in to your partner's expressive life. What can her behavior tell you about what's going on underneath the surface? Clues can be found through tone, body language, and verbal cues. Once you have a body of evidence, you will know whether to approach your mate or simply ride out the storm.

- Just ask. Sometimes your best guess won't get you the truth you need. But a quick and honest conversation can lead to happy attunement. Remember: Lead off with how *you* feel, and approach your partner with open-minded kindness. Also, choose an appropriate time to engage in a conversation that may become emotional. If you suspect tears will flow, a kind choice is to have your talk in private, rather than at a restaurant or park.
- Picture your spouse as a little child. This rarely fails to increase empathy for a loved one. When your partner is acting obnoxious or depressed and you feel you have no way to access his pain, imagine him as a five-year-old. (You can even glance at an old photo album to enhance this visual!) This simple trick may help you to access your kindness and approach him from a new vantage point.
- Practice laugh therapy. Use your sense of humor to gain access to your spouse's emotional life. Depending on the situation, a good five-minute chuckle can begin to break down walls. Shared laughter is relaxing, and the endorphins it produces allow good feelings to flow, increasing your chances for an open dialogue.

Chapter 18

Defusing a Bully

Ever since our days on the playground, we recognize a bully as someone who shames, berates, intimidates, or silences another person. In a marriage, if one spouse regularly bullies the other, the consequence is a partnership with little chance of long-term happiness.

Bullying, or what I call emotional tyranny, erodes a once-strong love. Statements such as "Why do I have to do everything around here?" and "What do you know?" confer blame and distaste. Insults like, "Are you really going to eat that?" and "Of course you don't know, idiot," round out a picture of a relationship gone sour. A less extreme example is the wife who persistently talks over her less verbal husband at a party. Emotional tyranny can wear many guises, but at its core is a feeling of discomfort about the self that causes the bully to lash out, in the hopes that the hurt lurking inside will be numbed or hidden or taken over by another. We must all learn to name whatever we are ashamed of. Once we can do this the sting of the bully loses its bite. Take five minutes a day to discuss with a trusted other what makes you uncomfortable. Putting shame into words reduces its toxicity.

A Bully's Shame

Understanding the difference between guilt and shame is key to clueing in on the inner workings of a tyrant. Although both emotional states can cause distress, shame's tentacles reach deep into the bowels of self-disdain, making one vulnerable to tyrannical tactics.

Helen Block Lewis, a Yale scientist and practitioner, wrote a landmark book in 1971 entitled *Shame and Guilt in Neurosis*. She maintains, "The experience of shame is directly about the self, which is the focus of evaluation. In guilt, the self is not central. . . . But rather the *thing* done is the focus." Guilt does not affect core identity as does shame, although both can be uncomfortable. I have always distinguished these two ideas by thinking of shame as "Something is wrong with me that I cannot change," such as being short, black, Jewish, etc. Guilt, however, is a violation of a boundary, as in: "I feel guilty I ate the last piece of pie." You can always commit to going to the gym or not eating the pie the next time around. But, shame makes you feel there is something about *you* that is worth hiding. Healing from shame's constricting grip requires exposure and the more you can put what you feel ashamed of into words, the less power it has over you.

Since the time of Lewis's book, there have been a multitude of studies measuring these reactions. In one conducted by June Price Tangney, the results indicated that when experiencing shame, participants were more likely to feel observed by others, and were concerned more about the opinions of others than their own self-perceptions. Shame was more likely to be accompanied by a sense of being inferior and physically small. Subjects reported a strong desire to hide from others when feeling shame in contrast to guilt. Also, when shamed, participants felt more isolated, less as though they belonged.

Shame-prone individuals appear more likely to blame others (as well as themselves) for negative events, are more prone to a seething, bitter, resentful anger and hostility, and are less able to empathize with others in general. Tangney notes: "Shame often motivates denial, defensive anger, and aggression." In other words, shame is what makes a bully a bully.

Shame and Empathy

The emotional tyrant berates his wife for attending a state university rather than a more prestigious school. We think, "How can he be so judgmental and hurtful?" And, more viscerally, "What a jerk!" But, if we were to look inside the mind of this bully, we would discover an interesting fact: He is unable to connect the words he is saying to the emotions they create in his wife. Emotional tyranny is the opposite of empathy. Indeed, the bully is overwhelmed by his own anxiety and shame (in this case, perhaps he feels intellectually inferior). The intensity of his own self-loathing blocks his ability to access his partner's emotions.

Empathy is defined as a shared emotional response between an observer and a stimulus person. For example, you observe that your partner lost out on a promotion. Empathy means you feel his disappointment and tell him how sorry you are that this oversight happened to him. If you feel it, he will feel it. Norma D. Feshbach, a Professor of Psychology at UCLA, suggests three skills that you can use to gain an empathic connection with your spouse.

First, consider another person's perspective. For example, say, "I understand that you do not like rock music, and even though I am passionate about it, I have bought tickets to the symphony for your birthday the same night my favorite band is playing at Madison Square Garden."

Then, learn to accurately recognize another's affective experience. For example, your spouse is sitting by herself during a party. You are aware that this is the anniversary of her father's death and she is not feeling like celebrating your friend's wedding anniversary even though you both showed up out of respect to them. You do not ask her to perk up, as you understand her loss.

Extra Credit
The next time you feel extremely frustrated by your spouse, resist the urge to act. Take five minutes to explore the situation and decide what *you* can do to create positive change. Keep in mind: You cannot change other people, only yourself.

Finally, you need to experience the range of emotions your partner is feeling. Imagine you recently moved into a new home. You are happy to finally have a place of your own, sad to leave your parent's house, scared to live so far out in the country, and worried that you will be lonely. You believe your partner is also happy to leave your parent's house for a home of your own, worried about the mortgage payments, thrilled to have his own workshop, overwhelmed by all of the work you have to do to get this place right.

Lacking the above cognitive and emotional skills, the bully stews in his own turmoil, blind to the pain he elicits in his spouse. It's a lonely place to be for both partners as you live your life on parallel tracks, rather than sharing a life.

How to Handle Your Bully

Emotional tyranny is akin to behaving like a toddler. There is very little impulse control in both cases. In addition, both the bully and the two-year-old lack the words to describe the depth of their frustration. For example, the bridezilla who is screaming that her dress is not the proper shade of champagne may think the issue is her attire. It is more likely that she is revealing her fear over the huge life change marriage brings.

If your spouse has bullying tendencies, it can be challenging to look past his offensive behavior to see the child screaming inside of him. No one deserves to be belittled or insulted, so why should you put up with it? Well, you don't take a toddler's temper tantrum personally, and you should take the same approach with bullies. If you have a long-term goal of staying in your marriage, it may take intensive patience and firmness in the beginning years.

SAY THIS
"I understand that something is bothering you that seems like it could be bigger than who last took the dog out. I love you and am here when you are ready to brainstorm what is truly going on with us beneath your frustration. I know for now you believe it is all about what is wrong with me, but I suspect there is more to it. I am happy to look at the part I play in the disconnect."

Establishing clear boundaries that keep your partner's hurtful behavior at bay can be achieved through interpersonal measures (changing the subject or lightening the mood), or by physically taking a break from the interaction. These five-minute fixes can help you resist reacting in anger or brittle silence when you are belittled or blamed by your partner. Approaching your partner with empathy and establishing clear boundaries of what is unacceptable behavior is the best beginning approach for keeping your marriage intact. Eventually, if nothing influences the bully to take charge of his destructive behavior (i.e., he is too trapped by his own limited view), you must be willing to walk away. But challenge yourself to keep in mind this demeaning stance toward you is not about you.

DANIEL & KAREN'S STORY

Daniel felt that his wife, Karen, didn't give him any emotional, intellectual, or social stimulation. They could drive for hours in the car with her saying nothing. He tried to start conversations about his ideas to fix the economy, his work on Wall Street, his friends, his passions. She would laugh a little, say "Oh, that's nice," and continue to be silent. Last week, visiting Karen's family, Daniel spent the evening noting to himself how dull her parents and her siblings were. On the way home, Daniel ranted and raved for the entire ride.

"All of you are stupid and weak. It must be genetic. How did I get stuck with you people? I must have been out of my mind!"

From Daniel's point of view, he provided a generous lifestyle for Karen, and felt he deserved someone who was better matched to his high energy. So what is Karen to do in this situation? She loved Daniel and suspected that his anger toward her is related to his shame, pain, and loss in childhood. His mother was depressed since his birth, and his father left the family after a violent exchange with Daniel when he was fourteen. Karen understood Daniel's emotional baggage, but she was also the victim of his verbal abuse.

Karen must learn to stand up for herself, to create boundaries that Daniel knows he cannot cross. She cannot dissolve or withdraw in the face of his unrelenting anger. Once they arrived home, Karen spoke up. "Daniel, you are my best friend. I love how interesting and alive you are. But, not everyone is like you. I am going to take a break from us tonight and stay across town with my sister. Feel free to call me there."

Karen chose to set up a boundary with love and not with anger, thus avoiding replicating his childhood trauma. She knew Daniel was an expert at expressing his anger and countering other people's anger. He was unused to being handled with compassion and love, which are the only powers that can disable the entrenched, truculent defenses developed by a smart, proud boy who was severely neglected. Daniel's tantrums were similar to those of a small child. He must learn to manage his rage, and realize that he projected childhood hurt onto his wife, and risked their long-term happiness.

If your spouse has bullying tendencies, your anger or fear can make it tempting to lash out in retaliation. But this strategy will only lead to an unhappy escalation. The better option is to set up boundaries that offer protection and teach your spouse that her behavior is unacceptable. In five-minute intervals, you can erect a flexible yet powerful bubble around yourself that prevents you from being sucked in to your spouse's shame-based actions.

- Change the subject. Imagine you are trapped in the car listening to your spouse go on and on about how she "does everything around here." Don't engage. Instead, introduce a topic you know will interest her. ("I have a juicy story about our new neighbor.") This is a quick fix, a virtual stop sign that says to your partner: "I refuse to engage in your harassment and am offering you a way out."
- Use humor. Making light fun of your partner—or yourself—can short-circuit a bully. If he claims he "does everything around here," respond with: "Oh, yes, and I sit around eating bonbons while you paint my toenails and give me head rubs. I can't work any harder, I'll chip my polish!" Humor can cut off a bully's rant because it shows that you are unwilling to accept his viewpoint, yet it is gentle enough to tap into his empathy. Laughter always helps to bring about connection.
- Take a break. If you sense your emotional tyrant is gaining momentum for a big rant, divert the situation by walking away. "I understand you're upset, but I think

it would be helpful for us to take a quick break and discuss this when emotions aren't so high." Take five minutes and pursue your own interest. Be careful not to become caught in an anger loop, arguing with your partner in your own head as you go about your activity. Take deep breaths and remind yourself that your bully is acting out due to his own shame and it really has little to do with you.

- Are you the bully? The next time you feel yourself becoming angry and accusatory toward your partner, have the discipline to stop for a few minutes and replay your behavior and motivations in your head. Are you really lashing out because she always embarrasses you in public? Or, is there some other reason you feel uncomfortable being out among other people? This exercise in self-awareness can feel challenging at first, but with practice you can curtail your own bullying tendencies—and create a stronger bond with your mate.

- Get underneath the surface. Ultimately, the hope is that whatever shame is simmering within you or your partner will come to light in a constructive manner. Take an educated guess and choose a good moment to broach the subject. Begin with your own feelings of shame. Then, when you have your partner's attention ask if you might guess about what could be his Achilles' heel.

Chapter 19

Resist Blaming

You are in charge of your own happiness. When you blame your spouse for your money problems, sex issues, feelings of neglect, or whatever is getting in the way of your well-being, you submit your power. Placing blame means making your destiny dependent on another person.

Why do we get caught in a cycle of blame? It can be difficult to resist pointing an accusatory finger at those closest to us. Living a full life means that challenges and interpersonal conflicts are inevitable. And, in fact, no one arrives in a marriage without a bag—or truckload—of emotional history. When life gets off track, it may initially be easier to blame your partner than it is to accept that blame yourself, but self-observation—an acquired skill—increases your opportunity to take partial responsibility for the problem. In contrast, reacting to stress by blaming your partner for the problem only leaves you trapped in your own bad feelings with no exit. Over time, faulting the other person without owning your part can thwart your once-happy union.

Blame Is a Mirror

Each time you blame your spouse for a problem, there is something within yourself that you are not facing. Blame is a mirror, reflecting back an image of yourself or your past that may be difficult to accept. For example, say you blame your money problems on your spouse: "She's so lazy, so lacking in ambition. Why can't she carry her weight around here?" The only thing blaming her for your financial insecurity accomplishes is to introduce negative feelings into your marriage. Trying to change someone's behavior through blame is a strategy with a poor track record for success. In addition, giving her total responsibility over a particular issue diminishes your power. What if she never changes? Do you really want to spend your life trapped inside your own anger and disappointment?

> ### *Extra Credit*
> During a quiet moment alone, take out a piece of paper and jot down three things for which you habitually blame your spouse. Now put it in a drawer. In the next day or two, re-examine what you wrote, noting the part you play in the situation. Keep this knowledge top-of-mind the next time a conflict arises and you are tempted to point a finger.

Instead, examine your past to explore your feelings about money. Was a lack of funds an issue growing up? How did your parents handle their financial life? Did your dad spend all his time at the office, leading you to believe that extreme ambition was the norm? Mine your rich personal history and become familiar with your assumptions about money.

By looking inside yourself, even for just five minutes a day, you are doing the hard work of increasing self-awareness.

Perhaps your private examination brings to light a hidden suspicion that *you* lack ambition. Seeing this quality in your partner reminds you of your secret fear. If this is the case, you can take steps to either eradicate or accept this aspect of yourself.

SAY THIS

"Honestly, my initial reaction is to blame you in this situation, but I want to avoid this by gaining a better understanding of *your* experience. What's your perspective?"

Giving up blaming or having unrealistically high expectations requires moving away from childhood dreams and into adult maturity. Once we truly enter the world of adulthood, we no longer flail and fight all of the responsibility that is part of being a grownup. In fact, we come to enjoy that we are finally the master of our own reactions to our fate, which gives us the ultimate access to a personal freedom. This freedom comes from self-knowledge because, although there is little you can do to alter your partner's behavior, you can change your own.

Take Personal Responsibility

The disempowering nature of blame can be overcome by empathy and action. First, reach out to your partner and connect on whatever issue is bothering you. Your blame may turn to empathy once you have an understanding of her experience. You may be surprised at what you discover. Say you've been blaming your partner because recently you've only been having sex once a month. Stewing in insecurity, you assume it's because she no longer finds you attractive. A simple conversation may teach you that, no, she thinks you are sexy beyond belief, but the new birth control pill she's on has diminished her sex drive. You won't know until you ask!

Once you better understand your partner's perspective, it's time to take action. Returning to our example above, regain your power by taking steps to improve your financial life—with or without your spouse's help. (You may have noticed a theme throughout this book: You can't change other people. The issue of blame highlights this fact.) You can choose to take charge by working longer hours, canceling the cable for a few months, or refinancing your home. There are plenty of options for improving your financial standing, and taking personal responsibility for your finances will augment your self-esteem as well as the size of your wallet. And, perhaps your actions will eventually influence your partner to get on board. See the table below for some ideas that may help you chip away at blame.

Blame Scenario	Personal Power Scenario
You and your spouse are both overweight. What can you expect, with the way she cooks?	Offer to go over the menu for the week and choose healthier options.
The kids never call, and you know why. Your husband is so critical of their lives!	Set up a once-a-week call with your kids, sometimes when your husband's there, sometimes when he's not.
He never touches me anymore. It's like we're roommates rather than lovers.	Introduce daily affection into your lives. A quick kiss or hug can bring a feeling of togetherness.
Your wife is alienating your conservative friends by talking about her new boob job.	Have a conversation with the goal of compromise. You love her openness, so don't crush it, but remind her that some people are more receptive to it than others.

Blame's Close Cousin: Expectation

Both blame and expectation lead to disappointment, and both originate within our own minds. In both scenarios, you don't check out where the other person is coming from. Instead, you create a scenario and then become disappointed if the other doesn't display the behavior that you've scripted for him.

Unattainable expectations—for yourself and for others—can lead to painful disappointment and defeat. Through an increase of self-love and, with it, empathy for your mate, you can come to know your own standards for right and wrong and what constitutes a good life. Frustration that your spouse is not doing what he should do is replaced by the reality of the way your life has turned out. By letting go of expectations, you give yourself the personal power to enjoy the life you have created.

The Power of Positivity

Blaming your spouse for your unhappiness is an extremely negative stance. After all, if your partner never changes you're stuck in a hole of your own making. Instead of sinking into negativity, take a positive, proactive approach when you need something. You could spend hours ruminating over how something is all your husband's fault, how you would have done it better, or how you wish he would change. Or, you can spend five minutes asking or planning for what you want. Do you feel he spends too many evenings at the office? Instead of blaming him for his neglect, offer to order take-out and join him for a meal there. It only takes a few minutes—and a change of heart—to reassess a situation through a more positive lens.

CORA & JAMES'S STORY

After almost fifty years of marriage, two children, and five grandchildren, Cora had just about had enough. Each time there was an opportunity for the kids to visit, James hemmed and hawed. He was too busy; they would make a mess. Cora's kids, James Jr. and Susan—and now her grandchildren—were her life! How could he deprive her of them? James enjoyed his two kids, but could live without the chaos of their broods. He liked dishing out career advice and talking golf, but felt lost and ignored while everyone admired the babies. He had lived through his share of diapers and teething, thank you very much.

Frequent visits had trickled down to the major holidays and Cora blamed her husband: "If you keep putting off their visits, our grandchildren aren't going to know us. This is your fault, and don't think I don't let Susan and James Jr. know it. They think you're a cranky old man."

How can Cora end this cycle of blame? After decades of marriage, she knew how stubborn her husband was, and that he wouldn't change. She was seemingly stuck. Or was she? Nothing was stopping Cora from taking charge of this situation—and getting what she wanted. Trying a new approach, she spoke to James one afternoon.

"I know you have your golf tournament next month, so I was thinking I would take that opportunity to fly out to visit the kids."

"You're going to fly on your own—without me? Won't they wonder where their grandfather is?"

"Look, you are welcome to join me. We could pick another weekend soon and go together. But, I'm not going to put off knowing my grandkids much longer."

"Fine. Enjoy."

Rather than wait, fuming, for James to make space in his life for the grandchildren, in five minutes, Cora took charge of her own happiness. Maybe James will join her; maybe he won't. But Cora could then focus on the positive elements of her marriage—his great sense of humor, his affection—that were being eclipsed by her blame. Remember: The more positively you approach your marriage, the more gratitude you'll have for what exists between you and your partner, and the less narrow-minded you'll be as to who is at fault when there is a conflict.

Blaming is so tempting in any long-term relationship. We blame our parents, our siblings, or our bosses—but most often it's our spouses who are caught in our crosshairs. Your intimate knowledge of your partner's strengths and weaknesses makes him vulnerable to your censure, but blaming others is not a path to happiness. Luckily, there are some five-minute, daily tricks that can alter your behavior. In just a few minutes, you can turn your negative stance into something positive.

- Stop trying to change your spouse. People aren't perfect—and think about how boring the world would be if we were! When you find yourself succumbing to blame, take a five-minute break (enjoy a bath, go jogging, etc.) and remind yourself that your partner is who he is and you chose him!
- Look in the mirror. The next time you're tempted to blame your spouse, take five minutes to meditate on the reasons that this particular issue resonates with you. Explore your past. Often, early experiences continue to affect us through the years. Do you find fault with your partner's tendency to be controlling because your mom was the same way? This interesting bit of insight can help you to recognize your sensitivity to this particular behavior. The next time you perceive your husband as being controlling, remind yourself to take a long cleansing breath, enjoy that he cares, laugh at your own defensiveness, and then do what you believe is correct.
- Approach your partner with empathy. Before you sink into an angry cycle of blame, engage him in a five-minute conversation about the issue at hand. Use the

lessons on body language from Chapter 12 to create an atmosphere of open communication. Ask nonjudgmental questions in order to make your spouse feel comfortable. You may be surprised by some mistaken assumptions. Most important: Never use the knowledge you gain from such a conversation as ammunition in a future argument. This erodes trust.

- Take action. When you find yourself in a situation in which you feel you are being deprived of affection, time, shared housework, and so on, stop blaming and *do something* to alter the scenario. Offer a five-minute backrub or go with your spouse on an errand in order to spend time together. The key is to stop waiting for your partner to do what you would like. Do it yourself!
- Ruminating about how your partner is wrong can feel addictive. After all, it's so satisfying to be right. The arguments you have over dinner don't make for a happy home, but the arguments you have in your own mind are even more destructive. ("He's so selfish." "How could he . . . ?" "I would never put him in this position!" etc.) You can ride that adrenaline train straight to unhappiness. Or, you can take five minutes to just stop. Train your brain to notice when it gets caught in a blame spiral, then, choose an activity that distracts you from blame, such as exercise or calling a friend.
- Commit to positivity. Stop the negativity of blame in its tracks by choosing to approach your marriage in a positive light. Instead of muttering to yourself all day how your spouse is disappointing you, remind yourself of all of his wonderful traits. He may be lazy or sarcastic, but he is also loving, with a great sense of humor. Enjoy your flawed, yet good-enough lover!

Chapter 20

Fighting Fair

Ideally, a happy marriage is free of conflict. Right? Not so much. Actually, most spouses that go the distance experience plenty of disagreements. No fighting means no resistance, and no resistance risks putting out the fire. Newness and excitement often require some bumpy preparatory exchanges, but partners who remain engaged with one another can be challenged and stimulated by their spouses' dissimilar ways of thinking or behaving. The resultant conflict may be unpleasant for the short-term, but over the course of a lifetime, it is part of the privilege of watching each other change and grow.

Fair vs. Unfair Fighting

How do we happily—or at least constructively—embrace conflict in our marriages? The key lies in understanding the difference between fair and unfair fighting. Fair fighting means engaging in a dispute without shaming the other person. Different fighting styles, such as one person relying on logic to make his case while the other passionately pleads as she fights back tears, can be part of the structure of the exchange. No matter the fighting styles of you and your partner, fair fighting will eventually bridge the distance and each of you will learn something new about the other, as well as a way to think more expansively.

SAY THIS

"I am concerned that this discussion is quickly deteriorating. I want us to resolve this issue, but I think we need a break. Let's meet back after I take a shower (or check my e-mail or get a cup of tea)."

Unfair fighting, on the other hand, means hitting below the belt or characterizing the other negatively. Engaging in personality assassination by yelling insults, shaming your spouse, or saying "you always" or "you never" places the other person in an inescapable box. These types of exchanges are not only futile for finding a meeting of the minds, but are also unproductive as the discussion dissolves into how to best hurt one another. Unfair fighting involves one or more of the following:

- Shaming your partner by noting some aspect of himself he is unable to change. ("You're so short. No wonder you've got a complex.")
- Invoking family members in the argument. ("You're just like your mother.")
- Judging from a place of superiority. ("People like you are so cheap.")
- Using an inaccessible third party to deliver an insult. ("Your sister said I could expect something like this from you.")
- Putting your spouse in a box. ("You always criticize me," or "You never listen.")

When emotions run high, it can be tempting to lash out in frustration. This is especially risky when there is much at stake (whether or not to have children, taking a pay cut to pursue a passion, how to care for elderly parents, etc.). If you feel your face getting hot and it's becoming difficult to breathe, take a five-minute break. Walking away may circumvent the urge to insult your partner.

The Risk of Avoiding Conflict

Avoiding disagreements can be as damaging to your marriage as unfair fights. Being willing to disagree about what you believe is important is generally preferable to staying silent and hoping for the best. As the years pass by, swallowing your opinion in the name of going with the flow can lead to resentment. This tends to occur if one partner is particularly verbal, while the other is less talkative. The quieter spouse may feel insufficiently proficient at debate, thereby choosing the more passive option of not speaking up. But, allowing your partner to unknowingly trample your desires not only results in the slow burn of bitterness, it also robs both of you of learning about who you really are, what you value, and what you need.

LUCIA & ANTONIO'S STORY

Lucia was born in Central America where civil war ensued for twelve years of her youth. She made an early childhood vow that there was no point to fighting. When she married Antonio she had her own clothing manufacturing business in her country. They eventually moved to New York for Antonio's corporate job, and Lucia set out to become the perfect wife. She learned how to cook, kept the house clean, and devoted herself to caring for her husband. She was not completely intellectually engaged, but was absorbing a new skill set and did not want any conflict as she was holding onto her childhood vow. Although she never asked, Lucia believed that Antonio did not wish for her to work.

Shortly after their move, Lucia suffered a miscarriage. She went through a depression where she did not want to leave the house. Following her recovery, Antonio asked for a divorce and moved out. He felt they didn't share the same values because she didn't work. Lucia was bereft. She had no idea Antonio did not want her to be a housewife as both of their mothers had been. Once he was gone, Lucia did not have the opportunity to have fair fights to work out their differences.

This is the disaster of not confronting your partner when you have the chance. Antonio did not have the positive feelings to sustain the marriage and he kept Lucia in the dark until a few weeks before he left. She, on the other hand, was mostly enjoying her role as housewife until she lost the baby. But with no dialogue this marriage was probably already over.

If we rewind this scenario back a year, was there a moment that could have changed the course of their marriage? Probably. Imagine the power of the following dialogue:

"Lucia, I know you are content cooking and cleaning for me, but these things matter much less to me than having a wife who is engaged in the world and has her own career goals. I feel like we have nothing to talk about at dinner these days."

"Why should I work if we don't need the money? I do so much for you—don't you appreciate it?"

"I fell in love with and married a businesswoman. Don't you miss the challenges and rewards of that life?"

"Yes and no. I had no idea you felt this way. I'll have to think about it. It can be hard finding a good balance between work and being home, especially if we want to have kids. But I'm glad to know how you feel."

Perhaps Lucia would have secured a part-time job, perhaps not. But Antonio's willingness to be honest and risk offending his wife would have given them the chance to bring this particular undercurrent to light.

Stand Your Ground

Fighting fair means keeping your boundaries in place. When you feel strongly about something, be persistent. Your determination can influence your partner to see where you are coming from. Some arguments do require lengthy discussions, but conflicts can often be resolved in several five-minute dialogues. The advantage is that brief engagements prevent things from becoming heated and devolving into unfair fights. Imagine that you feel your spouse has a tendency to make racist comments, which you deplore. Break down this potential conflict into three small discussions. First, bring it up in a personal way ("Prejudging an entire group of people makes me feel ashamed that you are my partner. What do you think it?"). Once you've spoken your piece and she's responded, walk away. Next, choose a moment when she is saying something disrespectful about a group of people and point it out to her ("You probably aren't even aware of it, but right now you are embarrassing me. I wish you would choose a more constructive way of communicating"). Finally, the next time you observe this behavior, make light of it, but let her know you noticed ("I love it when you are prejudiced, Darling. It makes me feel like I'm married to my racist old grandmother"). Breaking down this potential conflict into small segments may be more effective than having one big blow-out where you voice your thoughts, she says her piece, and that's that.

SAY THIS

"I want to understand where you are coming from, so I promise to listen to your point of view without interrupting. Please, go ahead."

Listening Builds a Bridge

You may feel that you are absolutely, positively right, but most conflicts have an element of subjectivity. Often, healthy resolution is a compromise that is a result of actively listening to one another's point of view. Tuning in to your partner during a clash can feel frustrating in the moment ("I know what he's going to say, and it's so off base!"), but you may be surprised at what you learn. Plus, listening is a show of good faith. During an argument, offer to take turns hearing each other out. One five-minute idea is for you to tune in and listen for a few minutes, then take a breather for another few minutes to absorb what was said. Repeat what you think you heard. If she says, "Yes, you got it," then switch roles.

Another way to ensure that you are being heard, and vice-versa, is to pause during a fight, take a five-minute break, and write down your perspectives. Reading your partner's thoughts on paper is a great way to listen to her point of view. Many people write more clearly than they speak in the heat of the moment, so this has the added advantage of bringing lucidity to your debate.

Extra Credit

A great way to enhance mutual understanding is to actually take the other's side in an argument. The next time you find yourself in a fight, pause and suggest to your partner you each take five minutes to argue the other person's perspective. This challenge may open your eyes and cut the fight short.

If your marriage were a tree, fighting fair would be the fertilizer that gives it a boost. You learn about each other's desires, what you each hold dear. You can both open up more and more, and your bond is strengthened by the increased awareness. For this reason, don't avoid disagreement or ruin a fair fight with shaming insults or characterizations. Embrace marital conflict and watch your tree grow.

Five-Minute Strategies

Fighting fair is a skill that, like any other, takes time and practice to perfect. Again, we employ the Golden Rule. If you don't want her to bring your withdrawn dad into the argument, don't bring up her alcohol-soaked mom. If you'd like her to listen, do the same. The following five-minute strategies can help you resist turning what could be a constructive disagreement into an ugly battle.

- In a heated argument, keep your struggle fair by taking five-minute breaks to regain your serenity. This will lessen the likelihood of either of you lashing out with insults or boxing the other in. It will also give you the opportunity to consider your spouse's point of view. Use this time to note how you tend to characterize your partner ("She is a control freak," or, "He always has to win"). And, then, throw these thoughts out the window by reminding yourself that people are more than just a collection of unchanging traits.
- Notice how your fair fights tend to be more productive than your shaming battles. Take a few minutes to think back over the course of your relationship. Can you recall a particularly damaging argument that didn't resolve much? Now consider a productive fight that you are proud of, even if it was uncomfortable at the time. Keeping these disparate fights in mind will help you avoid the temptation of an unfair clash in the future.
- Break down your dispute into five-minute segments. Employ different strategies each time you bring up the subject at hand: directness, sympathy, humor, etc.

Over time, you may influence your partner to enlarge his horizons. Plus, you will see which approach best reaches your spouse. Perhaps a direct approach will cause him to be defensive, but a bit of humor will soften him enough to begin to consider your side.

- Offer to listen to your partner without interrupting for five minutes. Swallow your "But wait . . . " and "That's crazy!" Repeat what you heard. Don't spend this time vaguely tuned in, planning out your response. Listen as if this discussion were a class and what he says is material that will definitely be on the final exam.

- If you have something on your mind, or desire a change in your partner's behavior, be willing to talk about it, even if it risks a fight. Remember: Arguments are a necessary part of a healthy and stimulating marriage. If you are conflict adverse, it can be helpful to take a few minutes to plan out what you will say in advance.

- Have your argument on paper. Spend five minutes jotting down your thoughts. Then, trade. You'll find that you are much less likely to insult your partner on paper than verbally in the heat of the moment. This also gives you time to absorb one another's positions before re-engaging.

Chapter 21

Hug Naked

Humor is a powerful tool to keep your marriage afloat—especially in times of difficulty. A thorny discussion can be softened by a smile, a laugh, or, if you're so inclined, a pratfall. A tense moment vanishes when you change the subject to light-hearted banter. Think back: Was there a plethora of smiles and laughter in the early days of your relationship? Keeping your sense of humor intact can resurrect those happy emotions and remind you that your spouse is the same person with whom you fell in love.

Perhaps you are thinking, "I am dealing with serious issues in my marriage. Are you really advising me to start making jokes?" Yes and no. You don't need to do a stand-up routine in the middle of your living room. But, infusing your marriage with laughter, even if it's sometimes rueful, prevents you and your partner from losing your connection. In happy times and hard times, the best defense is humor. Finding irony in everyday life, laughing and making other people laugh, is the most powerful way you can control your unpredictable destiny.

Laughter as Medicine

Laughter is a tranquilizer with no side effects. Medical studies show that, like exercise, it boosts levels of endorphins, the body's natural painkillers, and suppresses levels of epinephrine, the stress hormone. This fact is exploited by Laughter Yoga Clubs, the phenomenon that Indian physician Madan Kataria invented in 1995. Begun with a mere five people, there are now more than 6,000 clubs in sixty countries. People suffering from physical and emotional difficulties as well as those just looking for a lift, join together to take advantage of the healing power of laughter.

Author Norman Cousins explored the influence of laughter over twenty-five years ago when he wrote *Anatomy of an Illness*. Told that he had little chance of surviving a life-threatening tissue disorder, Cousins developed a recovery program incorporating megadoses of vitamin C, along with a positive attitude, and laughter induced by Marx Brothers films. Cousins writes, "I made the joyous discovery that ten minutes of genuine belly laughter had an anesthetic effect and would give me at least two hours of pain-free sleep." If laughter's power can heal the body and spirit, imagine what it can do for your marriage.

Moods Are Contagious

Recall a time when you were perfectly content and your stressed-out spouse entered the room. I'm sure it didn't take long for your shoulders to tense up and your mind to start racing, did it? Moods are contagious. This is good news when it comes to having a sense of humor because laughter is as infectious as a yawn. In addition, laughing with your spouse is more intense than laughing alone. Surprises that are embedded within safe contexts bring the irrepressible urge to laugh and share joviality with others. Mutual laughter signals that you find your current situation to be safe and lighthearted and that you'd like to use this time to build connections with your partner.

Extra Credit

Conduct the following experiment over the course of a week. First, approach your spouse while you are in a grouchy mood. How does he respond? Second, yawn and say how tired you are. Does he soon become droopy-eyed as well? Third, enter the room laughing big, hearty laughs. Watch as his surprise turns to joy and he joins in.

Even if you don't consider yourself to be a funny person, and your spouse's talents run more toward accounting than clowning around, there are ways to invite humor into your life. Spend an evening at your local comedy club or at the movies seeing the latest comedy. Notice as you walk out of the show how the shared experience of laughter makes you feel more connected and relaxed. Anyone can infuse daily life with mirth. For five minutes a day, commit to sharing the influence of hilarity with your partner. Here are some ideas to get you started:

- Dance in your living room. A little boogie or a little shimmy may light up your spouse's face even if it is just to make fun of how or what you two are doing. Making fun of ourselves is a very warm way to enjoy humor while together.
- Sing to him. Choose a song that has meaning for both of you then sing it like you're alone in the shower.

Maybe your performance wouldn't win you a spot on *American Idol*, but it could win your partner's smile. Again who cares if he is laughing with you or at you? Fun is fun.

- Laugh for no reason. You don't need to perform or tell a joke to engage in a mutual laugh fest. Amusement for no reason—or just at the joy of being alive—can alleviate stress and discord.
- Hug naked! Nothing will get you giggling like taking off your clothes and just hugging. It's intimate and, for some of us, silly, and may even lead to a happy bedroom encounter.

MAISEY & FRED'S STORY

Maisey and her ex-boyfriend, Al, reconnected on Facebook and gradually began speaking together on the phone. Al lives thousands of miles away and Maisey enjoyed their platonic phone conversations. Although Al is chronically ill, has never been able to support himself, and suffers from severe depression, he is very funny. But these calls made Maisey's husband Fred anxious and he asked her to cut off contact with Al.

From an outside observer, this situation has an innocent incongruity. Fred is handsome, athletic, devoted to Maisey and the children, and supports them generously. They share all of the same interests—golf, sports, food—and he is the darling of her extended family. So why would Maisey ever leave Fred for Al?

Fred's inability to take a lighthearted stance about these phone calls—or much of anything—was disrupting his connection to his wife. Fred was bothered by her giggles over the phone, because he couldn't remember the last time she laughed with him. The stress of being a cardiologist and raising two kids sent his sense of humor into hiding. After discovering a witty message from Al on Maisey's Facebook page, Fred had a choice: to trust his wife and laugh with her, or to stifle her joy at rediscovering an old friend. In a moment of clarity, Fred tried the former.

"Your computer was open to your Facebook page, and I couldn't help but read what Al wrote. It's amazing the things that happen to this guy!"

"I know. He really does get into some wild situations. Listen, I know my contact with Al makes you uncomfortable, but please trust me. You'd like Al. He's dark, but hilarious. He told me once that in high school he used to wear fangs to the mall and scare unsuspecting ladies. He's a weirdo and totally not my type. It's strange that we dated for that brief time."

"It's not Al that upsets me, Maisey. It's just that between work and everything, I can't remember the last time we really laughed together. I miss that. I don't know where that went."

"You're right. Let's both make an effort to see the lighter side of things. Why don't we start by sending the kids to my mom's this weekend? We can rent a bunch of comedies, drink some wine, and stay up too late."

"That sounds amazing."

As for Maisey and Fred's situation, it often happens that reality gets in the way of fun. It's usually easy to be carefree in the beginning of marriage because the weight of life's more difficult moments has yet to be borne. But, especially for couples in their forties, the perfect storm of career pressures, raising young children, and caring for aging parents can kill mirth. That said, what are we doing all of this for if there's no joy to be had? It takes a conscious effort to prioritize laughter. Remember that humor has the power to ease anxiety and discord, not only by augmenting your connection with your mate, but also by altering your physical state for the better.

SAY THIS

"Let's play a game. When we get home tonight, let's each have a funny story to tell the other about something that happened today. If nothing amusing happens, let's make it happen!"

Make a commitment to laugh with your partner five minutes a day. Be creative. It can be anything from watching a funny YouTube video together to greeting him wrapped only in cellophane, a rose between your teeth. The sky's the limit!

Five-Minute Strategies

Don't underestimate the power of laughter. It may seem juvenile at first glance, especially if your marriage is going through a dark time due to joblessness, infidelity, or illness. By advising humor, I am not making light of the seriousness of marital discord. But I am trying to point out the power of maintaining your sense of humor. It's a ray of light, a breath of fresh air, that's especially necessary when tension is high. Humor is a quick fix, and there are as many five-minute ways to make someone laugh as stars in the sky. You know what elicits a smile in your partner. Commit today to making it happen.

- Notice how your moods are contagious. Take five minutes to engage your partner in laughter instead of walking into the room complaining about what happened that day. Make a joke, tell a funny anecdote, or just laugh for no reason. Your spouse will likely match your lightheartedness.
- Take a few minutes to check out the entertainment section in your local paper. Is something funny happening in town like a new Judd Apatow movie at the theater? Or, is Jerry Seinfeld in town? Invite your spouse to join you.
- It doesn't take long for infectious laughter to take hold. Surprise your mate by singing, dancing, or basically being silly around the house. Let go of any self-consciousness! After all, this is the person who knows

and loves you best. He'll likely take delight in seeing a lighter side of you.

- As you struggle with life's inevitable pain, enjoying the small, subtle experiences of every day can fade away without our even noticing. Have a five-minute conversation with your partner and make a mutual commitment to start your own private laughing club. Promise to laugh together at least once a day, for five minutes, no matter what is happening in your lives. It may sound juvenile, but shared laughter with your spouse is a magical elixir.

Conclusion

Since antiquity, many philosophers have considered happiness subjective. But self-honesty is not. Three thousand years ago in Greece, Mencius stated, "There is no greater joy than to find on self-examination, that I am true to myself." Immanuel Kant backs up this point: "It is the highest maxim, uninhibited truthfulness towards oneself as well as in the behavior towards everyone else is the only proof of a person's consciousness of having character."

Practicing psychotherapy for the last forty years has taught me that there is an objective nature to happiness in a marriage. Happiness is connected to self-honesty as well as kindness and authenticity toward one's partner. Specific actions taken and received create mutual contentment.

It is not uncommon that when a marriage ends, it is because one of the partners has not alerted her spouse to her unhappiness. By the time the clueless one finds out, it is too late. The teachings in this book instruct you to never be caught unaware. Taking your own and your spouse's temperature on a regular basis, for just five minutes a day, is essential for keeping your union alive and well.

The strategies throughout this book can turn almost any relationship from one of frustration and isolation to warmth and connection. In my office recently, I reinforced for myself the legitimacy of this claim. A newly engaged couple came to see me. I had worked for almost a year with the man, until he felt sure enough to buy the ring and asked his partner to marry him. He was now ready to commit to her for life. But, after begging him to get engaged for three years, she was unsure. Why? Because she often felt alone when they were together. He was continuously on his Blackberry, connecting to his office or to his family members. I asked him if he would consider turning off the device while they had dinner or for at least one hour during their evenings together. He flatly refused, saying, "I have elderly parents and a business that needs me until 11 P.M. every evening."

I was beginning to feel as defeated as his fiancé. Then I looked at her closely and a light bulb went off. She had moved here from California after her older brother had been killed. She only had her fiancé as her closest confidant, while he had an army of friends and relatives at his beck and call. So I asked him if he would, for five minutes every day, ask his darling about the specifics of her childhood, about her brother, her school friends, her relatives, her neighborhood. Just five minutes a day devoted entirely to his beloved to discuss some piece of her past. In this way, her history would be brought into the present, her roots would come alive, and she would feel less like an orphan. She was thrilled with this idea and he found it simple to do. They came in tense and left the office beaming.

What does this tale tell us? Yes, we are buffeted by experiences beyond our control. In addition, the research of psychologist Sonja Lyubomirsky, author of *The How of Happiness, A Scientific Approach to Getting the Life You Want*, informs us we are all born with a set point for happiness. Lyubomirsky reports that 50 percent is our set point, that 10 percent is what happens to us, and 40 percent is within our domain to influence. This book is dedicated to the 40 percent that you can control. You become who you are by how you respond to the changing situations in your life. To be happy in your marriage, you need to find the balance between empathy for your partner and your own capacity for resilience that you'll need to bounce back from life's adversities.

Neurophysiologist Felicia Huppert uses brain science to show how set points for happiness vary for individuals depending on the person's temperament and emotional style. She says that the genes within each individual need to be turned on or turned off by modifying circumstances, attitudes, and behaviors. This is exactly the premise of *Save Your Marriage in Five Minutes a Day*. Devote a small part of each day to caring for your marriage and turn on your happy genes as well as your partner's.

Daily awareness of the state of your relationship increases the chance that you will experience gratitude. This gives you the best chance of living happily ever after. After all, life is not a fairy tale unless you try your best to make it one. Five minutes a day is all it takes to set sail toward your best shot at bliss.

You may have noticed a repeated sentiment in this book: You can't depend on anyone else for your happiness. If nothing else sticks after you finish this book, my wish for you is to take the phrase to heart. It will increase your compassion toward others as well as toward yourself.

So I leave you with a prayer that you develop an open heart to all of the people you love—including yourself.

References

Allen, Elizabeth S., and Galena K. Rhoades. "Not All Affairs Are Created Equal." *Journal of Sex & Marital Therapy* 34, no. 1 (January 2008): 51–65.

Bird, Chloe E., "Gender, Household Labor, and Psychological Distress: The Impact of the Amount and Division of Housework," *Journal of Health and Social Behavior* 40 (March 1999): 32–45.

Blanchflower, David G., and Andrew J. Oswald, "Money, Sex and Happiness: An Empirical Study," *Scand. J. of Economics* 106, no. 3 (2004): 393–415.

Block Lewis, Helen. *Shame and Guilt in Neurosis.* New York: International Universities Press, 1971.

Bok, Sissela. *Exploring Happiness.* New Haven: Yale University Press, 2010.

Costello, C. G. (Ed.). "Shame and Guilt" in *Symptoms of Depression.* New York: Wiley, 1993.

Cousins, Norman. *Anatomy of an Illness*. New York: W. W. Norton & Co., 1995.

Damasio, Antonio. *The Feeling of What Happens: Body and Emotion in the Making of Consciousness*. New York: Harcourt, 1999.

Driver, Janice L., and John M. Gottman, "Daily Marital Interactions and Positive Affect During Marital Conflict Among Newlywed Couples," *Family Process* 43, no. 3 (2004): 301–314.

Ebrahim, S., et al., "Sexual Intercourse and Risk of Ischaemic Stroke and Coronary Heart Disease: The Caerphilly Study," *Journal of Epidemiology Community Health* 56, (2002): 99–102.

Ecker, B., and B. Toomey, "Detentiation Differentiation of Symptom-Producing Implicit Memory in Coherence Therapy," *Journal of Constructivist Psychology* 21, no. 2 (2008): 87–150.

Ekman, Paul, and Richard Davidson. *The Nature of Emotion: Fundamental Questions*. NY, Oxford University Press, 1994.

Feshback, N. D., and S. Feshbach. *Aggression and Altruism: A Personality Perspective*. In C. Zahn-Waxler, E. M. Cummings, and R. J. Lannotti (Eds.). *Altruism and Aggression: Biological and Social Origins*. Cambridge, UK: Cambridge University Press, 1986.

Fonagy, P. "Multiple Voices vs. Meta-Cognitions: An Attachment Theory Perspective," *Journal of Psychotherapy Integration* 7 (1997): 181–194.

Fosha, Diana. *The Transforming Power of Affect*. New York: Basic Books, 2000.

Gilbert, Daniel. *Stumbling on Happiness*. New York: Vintage, 2007.

Goleman, Daniel. *Emotional Intelligence: Why It Can Matter More Than IQ*. New York: Bantam Books, 10th Anniversary Edition, 2006.

Huppert, Felicia A., Nick Baylis, and Barry Keverne (Eds.). *The Science of Well-Being*. Oxford: Oxford University Press, 2007.

Jacobson, Bonnie, PhD. *Choose to Be Happily Married, How Everyday Decisions Can Lead to Lasting Love.* Boston: Adams Media, 2010.

———. *If Only You Would Listen.* New York: St. Martin's Press, 1995.

———. *Love Triangles.* New York: Crown Publisher, 1993.

———. *The Shy Single.* New.York: Rodale Press, 2004.

Kant, Immanuel. *Foundation of the Metaphysics of Morals.* (L.W. Beck, Trans.) Indianapolis, IN: Bobbs-Merrill, 1959/1785.

Kashdan, Todd B., and John E. Roberts, "Trait and State Curiosity in the Genesis of Intimacy: Differentiation from Related Constructs," *Journal of Social and Clinical Psychology* 23, no. 6 (2004): 792–816.

Kashdan, Todd B. *Curious?* New York: HarperCollins, 2009.

Levey, B. R., M. D. Slade, et al., "Longevity increased by positive self-perceptions of aging," *Journal of Personality and Social Psychology* 83 (2002): 261–70.

Lyubomirsky, Sonja. *The How of Happiness: A Scientific Approach to Getting the Life You Want.* New York: Penguin Press, 2008.

Main, M. "Recent Studies in Attachment: Overview with Selected Implications for Clinical Work." In Goldberg, S. R. Muir, and J. Kerr (Eds.), *Handbook of Attachment: Theory, Research and Clinical Applications.* Hillsdale, NJ: Analytic Press, 1995.

Miller, S., and E. Byers, "Actual and Desired Duration of Foreplay and Intercourse: Discordance and Misperceptions Within Heterosexual Couples," *Journal of Sex Research* 41, no. 3 (2004): 301–309.

Rankin-Esquer, Lynn A., Charles K. Burnett, Donald H. Baucom, and Norman Epstein, "Autonomy and Relatedness in Marital Functioning." *Journal of Marital and Family Therapy* 23, no. 2 (April 1997): 175.

Schore, A. N. *Affect Regulation and the Repair of the Self.* New York: Norton, 2003.

Schutte, N. S, J. M. Malouff, C. Bobik, T. D. Coston, C. Greeson, et al. "Emotional Intelligence and Interpersonal Relations," *The Journal of Social Psychology* 141, no. 4 (2001): 523–535.

Smith, George Davey, S. Frankel, J. Yarnell. "Sex and Death: Are They Related? Findings from the Caerphilly Cohort Study," *British Medical Journal* 315 (1997): 1641–4.

Smith, K. M., P. A. Freeman, and R. B. Zabriskie, "An Examination of Family Communication Within the Core and Balance Model of Family Leisure Functioning," *Family Relations* 58 (2009): 79–90.

Wallerstein, Judith. *The Unexpected Legacy of Divorce: A 25-Year Landmark Study.* New York: Hyperion, 2000.

—"The Unexpected Legacy of Divorce: Report of a 25-Year Study," *Psychoanalytic Psychology* 21, no. 3 (2004): 353–370.

Weeks, David J., "Sex for the Mature Adult: Health, Self-Esteem and Countering Ageist Stereotypes," *Sexual and Relationship Therapy* 17, no. 3 2002): 231–240.

Weigel, D. J., "A Dyadic Assessment of How Couples Indicate Their Commitment to Each Other," *Personal Relationships 15* (2008): 17–39.

INDEX

About the Author

Bonnie Jacobson, PhD, earned her doctorate at New York University where she is currently an adjunct professor in the Applied Psychology department. She is also the director of The New York Institute for Psychological Change; one of the founders of Elem, a not-for-profit organization that works with youth in distress in Israel; and is a specialist in modern analytic group therapy. Dr. Jacobson is also a media expert who is frequently called on by television, radio, newspapers, and magazines to discuss topics related to relationships. She lives in New York City with her husband and her immediate family lives throughout the world in Philadelphia, London, San Francisco, Washington, D.C., Santa Fe, Israel, Zurich, and Hallendale, Florida; a fact that supports her passion for traveling.

jane
ON TOP

Getting Where Women Really Belong

- Trying to lose the losers you've been dating?
- Striving to find the time to be a doting mother, dedicated employee, and still be a hot piece of you-know-what in the bedroom?
- Been in a comfortable relationship that's becoming, well, too comfortable?

Don't despair! Visit the Jane on Top blog—your new source for information (and commiseration) on all things relationships, sex, and the juggling act that is being a modern gal.

Sign up for our newsletter at
www.adamsmedia.com/blog/relationships
and download a **Month-ful of Happiness!**
That's 30 days of free tips guaranteed to lift your mood!